Thanksgiving

The **power** to **transform** your life

Book Four

A daily devotional to bring you into the presence of God

Stella Doggett

Published by
The Centre for Life Management
172 Long Street,
Dordon, England.
B78 1QA
www.lifetraining.co.uk

Copyright © Stella Doggett 2023

nless otherwise indicated all scripture quotations are taken from the New International Version, Copyright © 1978 New York International Bible Society, published in the UK by Hodder & Stoughton.

RSV. Revised Standard Version, Copyright © 1946,1952 The division of Christian education of the national council of the churches of Christ in the USA.

AMP. The Amplified Bible, Expanded Edition Copyright © 1987 Zondervan Corporation and The Lockman Foundation.

TPT. The Passion Translation, New Testament with Psalms, Proverbs, and Song of Songs Copyright © 2018 Broadstreet Publishing group, LLC

NASB. New American Standard Bible Copyright © 1995 The Lockman Foundation.

The Message. Copyright © 2004 by Eugene H. Peterson.

AV. King James Authorised Version.

The emphasis in scripture references using bold type has been mine.

ISBN 978-1-7392333-3-4

Cover design by Sian James @cre8sian_art@yahoo.com
Typeset by Angela Selfe
Project managed by theweddedhare@gmail.com

Acknowledgements

I would like to thank all those who have helped me to complete all four of these daily Devotional Books including those who have sent me their encouraging feedback from Books One, Two and Three.

Once again my wonderful and patient husband Mark, my 'joint heir of the grace of life', (1 Peter 3:7, AMP.) has faithfully and patiently encouraged me, edited, and checked both the biblical references and context of these daily readings. He has also written several of these daily reflections himself, by way of encouraging me to take a Sabbath rest from the initial daily writing. Your support, practical and spiritual, has been amazing and yet again I have to say that without your company on our journey of life with Jesus, these readings would have been far less rich and may never have seen the light of day.

Thanks also to our fellowship group here in Dordon, and for other friends those who have partnered with this project in prayer and encouragement, Thanks again to John who has continued to faithfully 'proof read' each of the 'Days', and to Fi who joined the proof reading team.

Because these 'Daily Meditations' were originally written over the course of the year Days 350 to 358 cover the Christmas season. The thoughts contained within them are of course applicable throughout the year but as you read through this book please feel free to put them to one side until the appropriate time.

Introduction

When I first started to write these devotional blogs in 2021, it was because I felt that the Lord was saying that He wanted to shift the mindset of His people into one of gratitude; a mindset that would help us to move into a lifestyle that would lead us into revival and sustain us through times of shaking. I felt that the Lord was telling me that He would give me an encouraging word around 'Thanksgiving' for every day of the year if I would write it down and post it, and He did!

Three hundred and sixty five blogs on this one topic, one for every day of the year, seemed like a big ask, but God faithfully gave me something to write every day and when I started I had no idea how blessed I myself would be by doing so. I was then encouraged by friends to publish these blogs as a daily devotional book and it was not until I came to design the cover, with my friend Sian, that the title for the books became clear – Thanksgiving - the Power to Transform your Life.

I think it is only now, having edited these blogs over the past two years, in order to publish them, that I am fully grasping why the Lord had insisted on 365 meditations, and it was this: To turn something from a good idea into the habit of a lifetime takes time and persistence.

Now I have heard it said that it takes forty days to break an old habit and form a new one, but in walking through this year of daily 'thanksgiving' meditations we are not just forming a new habit, we are changing our mindset and we are also battling with the spiritual atmospheres all around us, and within our own fallen human nature. The Lord knew that we would need a reminder every day for at least a year to really transform our thinking.

I have therefore been so blessed by the feedback from various readers who have said that these books have been really helpful because they have indeed needed a reminder *everyday* to step into this thanksgiving lifestyle. I also have to confess that, as I have re- read them (several times for editing purposes) I myself have, on many occasions, been in need of such reminders.

Thanksgiving does so much for us. It doesn't just make us nicer people to be around it also keeps us from pride, forgetfulness and entitlement in the good times, and discouragement, cynicism and a sense that 'I can't make it' in the tough ones. It becomes a daily source of joy. Remember Jesus was anointed with joy above all his fellows. (See Hebrews 1:9). I now also realise that 'Thanksgiving' is one of the greatest and most profound ways of releasing the powerful grace of God into our lives.

I would encourage you to 'imitate those who through faith and patience inherit what has been promised.' (Hebrews 6:12) because a big ingredient in our maturing as Christians is 'perseverance.' James encouraged the Christians of his time with the words, 'As you know, we consider blessed those who have persevered. You have heard of Job's perseverance and have seen what the Lord finally brought about. The Lord is full of compassion and mercy.' (James 5:11).

We need those daily reminders that will help us to persevere with giving thanks 'in the midst of everything' (See 1 Thessalonians 5:18, TPT). Character and maturity come as we make the right choices, and the choice to come into the Lord's presence with thanksgiving in all our circumstances is a way of surrendering my life daily into His hand: the best, the good and the difficult parts. **You see 'thanksgiving' wraps everything up in the grace of God**, and it is the most profound strategy in the middle of the toughest of situations. Even more importantly, 'Thanksgiving never fails to delight the heart of God.'

As before on each day you will find a suggested activation. Personalising these suggestions will help you to be a 'doer' of the word and not just a 'hearer', (James 1:22). So please use these reflections in your own way, and let the Holy Spirit bless you and fill you as you 'Enter His Gates', and find Him to be all that you need. I pray that this journey of 365 days will transform your relationship with the Almighty, and hence your life!

Enjoy!!

DAY 275 | The Sacrifice of Thanksgiving and Reaching God's Heart

As we start on the fourth quarter of our 'Year of Thanksgiving', Psalm 50 has some very helpful insights for pilgrims who are hungry to pursue this journey. In it God is telling His people that He doesn't need the sacrifices of bulls and goats, because all the world is His and He has all He needs. He doesn't rebuke His people for these sacrifices and burnt offerings that are ever before Him (verses 7-13), but He does, however, invite them to "sacrifice thank offerings." (verse 14). It seems to me that the Lord is reminding His people that, although He owns the world, and has everything He needs, **He still loves to receive the sacrifice of thanksgiving**.

Simply put the Lord is delighted every time one of His children thanks Him for something. It is just so important for us not to downplay how much our thanks means to the Lord. Has saying 'grace' before a meal become routine? Well a good antidote to that is to practice **not** taking things for granted by cultivating the attitude of gratitude for all sorts of things throughout each day, like my eye sight, my freedom to travel, my work etc. It's so important for us to remember how thrilled the Lord is when we thank Him for every gift He gives us and not just the lasagne we had for tea today.

More than that, these verses (14-15) tell us that the Lord recognises that thanksgiving in challenging circumstances costs us something. He understands that it is not always easy to say "Thank You", and it thrills Him when we decide to do so. In 1 Chronicles 21:24 David says "I will not take for the Lord ... or sacrifice a burnt offering that costs me nothing." That sacrificial heart attitude is, I believe, something that delights the Lord, just as it would in our human relationships.

This psalm is a little goldmine for thanksgiving pilgrims like us – verse 15, continuing the sentence started in verse 14, says "and call upon me in the day of trouble, I will deliver you and you will honour me". This sounds like a cycle of blessing: as we offer a sacrifice of thanksgiving in today's challenging circumstance and we call for His help, the Lord says He will respond and come to deliver us. This then gives rise to more thanksgiving – "you will honour me."

It reminds me of Paul's words in Philippians 4:6, 'In everything by prayer and petition, with thanksgiving, present your requests to God,' And just in case we haven't got the message yet, the psalmist and the Holy Spirit remind us in the last verse (23) of Psalm 50, 'He who sacrifices thank offerings honours me, and he prepares the way so that I may show him the salvation of God.' What a beautiful thought that we can honour God – the all mighty, awesome, all sufficient one – who needs nothing – with our 'simple' sacrifices of praise.

In addition to what I do and how I live, what comes out of my mouth in praise and thanksgiving is so important. In addition to honouring the Lord in how I live, offering my thanksgiving does something in me, it's a way of preparing myself to see more of the salvation and deliverances that our super generous, loving, kind, giving God, (you can't out give Him) has brought, and wants to go on bringing, into my heart, life, and circumstances. This becomes a little clearer in the AV translation of Psalm 50:23 which reads, 'Whoso offereth praise glorifieth Me, and to him that ordereth his conversation aright will I show the salvation of God.'

Activation...

Let's ask the Holy Spirit, our God given helper, the one who comes alongside us, to remind us in the midst of our challenges, to take every opportunity to give thanks, especially when 'giving thanks' is a sacrifice. Remind yourself that this is a wonderful way of honouring God as you express and build your faith in His goodness and love.

Then keep a look out for His deliverances because they will follow and may well come in unexpected ways.

DAY 276 | The Sacrifice of Thanksgiving that Opens the Door for Deliverance

Before we leave Psalm 50 there is one more thought to encourage us. We mentioned yesterday the Lord's delight when one of His children thanks Him for something, and how important it is for us not to downplay how much our thanks means to Him. We recognised that in challenging circumstances thanksgiving will cost. That's the meaning of 'sacrifice'. Now we usually think of saying thank you when we are given something, so a 'sacrifice' of thanksgiving is akin to 'paying it forward.' It's gratitude in advance and a sign of our faith in God's commitment to us. It is not emotional blackmail, or an attempt to make God do what we want! We are **not** saying, "If I keep thanking God enough in this situation, He'll just have to do what I want." We are simply expressing our faith that He will.

In verse 23 of Psalm 50 we read, "He who sacrifices thank offerings honours me, and **he prepares the way so that I may show him the salvation of God.**" In this instance salvation is not so much about having our sins forgiven as about deliverance from difficult circumstances. Giving sacrificial thanks in a difficult situation is not about Him being a 'helicopter Dad', coming to extract us from difficulty without us necessarily doing anything ourselves, (although at times He will); it's about opening the door for the Lord to come and show us His way forward or maybe His way out.

These verses remind me again of Psalm 24:7,8, 'Lift up your heads O you gates; be lifted up, you ancient doors, that the **King of glory may come in**. Who is this King of glory? The Lord strong and mighty in battle, the Lord mighty in battle.' Now we have spoken on previous days about the rejoicing, praise and joy, which heralded the King's arrival at the gates of Jerusalem, at which sound the gates were opened to welcome Him in. In the same way I believe throwing back our heads in laughter, praise, and thanksgiving in a difficult situation, 'opens up' the doors of our heart, mind and spirit, by faith. This thanksgiving welcomes our King, 'mighty and strong in battle', to come and fight for us, in us and with us, with His might and power.

As we welcome Him with our thanksgiving, His powerful presence may be manifest in different ways, and always the choice is His. Sometimes, as with Shadrach Meshach and Abednego, He goes with us through the fire. (See Daniel 3:24,25). At other times, as with Paul, He bursts the prison open and we are free. (Acts 16:22-30). Sometimes He comes giving us wisdom as He did with Solomon, (1 Kings 3:16-27), and at other times he gives us grace to hold our ground in the face of persecution and even death like Stephen. (Acts 7:54-59). (N.B. Death can come in many forms not just physical, like the death of our reputation, or our way of doing something.)

Always He will manifest His presence by using that same situation to change us one more degree into the likeness of Jesus! (2 Corinthians 3:18). Often God doesn't deliver us immediately because He is working some good things into our lives through that situation. James 1:2-4 would encourage us that giving thanks, like 'considering it pure joy', helps us not to fight the Lord over His dealings with us, but to cooperate with Him and see the change that He wants to bring in us, before He changes the situation itself.

Returning to verse 23 of Psalm 50, when we are in need of a deliverance let us make our sacrifice of thanks, and thereby open the doors for the Lord 'strong and mighty' to come in. Then let Him show us how that deliverance is going to look. This can happen for us as individuals, and is also true for communities. When Israel was in trouble, and the armies of Moab, and Ammon were circling, the battle was won as they sent out the singers before the army. The song that they sang was nothing too complicated. It was simply, 'Give thanks to the Lord for He is good, for His love endures for ever'. (2 Chronicles 20:20-23). And God moved powerfully on their behalf.

Activation...

Give your sacrifice of thanks and praise today not to manipulate God into doing what you want Him to do, but as an act of great faith and surrender. By doing so you will 'honour' the Lord and bring Him great delight. By giving thanks and praise you are saying to the Lord, "I love you. I believe that you love me and are with me. I am welcoming you in to deal with this situation, in whatever way you choose, and I am giving you thanks now because you are faithful and you are good".

DAY 277 | Thanksgiving and Singing

I think singing must be very important to the Lord. Reading through the Bible it becomes clear that, whenever anything eventful happens, when ever God acts, or is present with His people, there is singing. We know that there was singing at creation for example because one of the first questions that the Lord asked Job was, "Where were you when I laid the earth's foundation? ... while the morning stars sang together and all the angels shouted for joy?" (Job 38:4-7). What an amazing moment that would have been. Then there were the angels singing joyfully to the Shepherds at Jesus birth, "Glory to God in the highest realms of heaven!" (Luke 2:14, TPT).

When Isaiah was foretelling the wonders of the coming salvation he declared, 'In that day you will say: "Give thanks to the Lord, ... Sing to the Lord, for He has done glorious things; ... Shout aloud and sing for joy, people of Zion, for great is the Holy One of Israel among you." (Isaiah 12:4-6). The sound of singing in heaven itself must be wonderful and totally awesome as, around the throne, the twenty four Elders, joined by millions upon millions of angels, sing very loudly, "Worthy is the Lamb, who was slain, to receive power and wealth and wisdom and strength and glory and honour and praise!" (Revelation 5:12). I think God likes a song!

We know from the many exhortations in scripture, that singing blesses the heart of God, (Psalm 33:1-3). Singing is also a wonderful gift to us His created beings. We are made in such a way that singing benefits us physically, emotionally and spiritually. Singing, like laughter, will physically release the endorphins that can lift our mood. Singing, especially if we are singing praise, or the truth about God, will also fill our minds and touch our emotions with uplifting thoughts and feelings, anchoring us again in His word and promises. And singing also plays a significant role in releasing the promised 'rivers of living water' from our innermost being, (John 7:37-39), so that our natural mind and emotions are flooded with revelation, insight, faith and trust.

My testimony is that, having been a Christian for over fifty years, I was feeling that my spiritual life had more or less reached a plateau. Then Matt Redmond's song '10,000 Reasons'[1] echoed around the world, and I felt the Lord challenge me with the words, 'Sing like never before, Oh my soul'. As

I did that, and set my heart to sing and worship every day, I was amazed as new revelation started coming to me like never before and old truths became alive and fresh.

Even if we have appreciated the gift of singing in our own lives and the spiritual life of the church, we probably still have no real idea of the powerful effect that singing our praise to the Lord has on our world spiritually; on the spiritual atmosphere all around us. I have no doubt that, just as the Lord loves our singing, the devil hates it, and that while our singing attracts the angelic forces into our lives like a magnet, it also repels the darkness and the spiritual forces that serve 'the prince of the power of the air'. (Ephesians 2:2, NASB).

Interestingly Isaiah, on several occasions, encourages singing **before** the deliverance comes. For example, 'Burst into songs of joy together, you ruins of Jerusalem...' (Isaiah 52:9). And let us not forget King Jehoshaphat who sent the singers out in front of his army when they were faced with overwhelming odds. (2 Chronicles 20:13-23). Needless to say they won a great victory that day. We can also read of Paul and Silas singing and praying in their prison cell **before** the earthquake comes and they are released and people saved. (Acts 16:22-34).

We can see from these examples that, not only is singing a wonderful gift, it is also a powerful spiritual weapon. Clearly the devil would like to keep us silent, but don't ever stop singing. Always remember that even if no pre written song comes to mind you can sing in the Spirit by making up your own song in your own language as David frequently did, or by singing in tongues. (1 Corinthians 14:15). Stay grateful for this wonderful gift.

Activation...

Singing out our praise and worship draws us into the presence of God like nothing else. So be continually thankful for this beautiful gift. The more you can appreciate what an amazing God given gift singing is, the more determined you will be to use it, and the more you do, the more your faith will grow. (Just remember you are singing to the Lord and not 'Britain's Got Talent' so don't let any 'lie' like, 'But I can't sing', stop you!!)

DAY 278 | Thanksgiving that there is Always More

We wrote yesterday about the blessing that singing is. It's a gift from God that releases a fresh spirit of revelation to us whereby old truths become richer in meaning and more powerful on our journey of transformation. One of those truths is this – there is always *more* with God. There is always *more* revelation for us to receive, *more* to learn and understand, *more* to grasp of His infinite wisdom, *more* to fathom of His boundless love, and *more* of His power and presence to experience. He truly is beyond anything we can imagine in our wildest dreams. And the good news is that not only is there *more of,* and *more to* God, but He Himself is highly delighted when He sees in us that hunger for *more*, in whatever area we are needing *more* of Him.

With God we will never ever find ourselves in an Oliver Twist like scenario, where we are 'told off' for wanting *more*. On the contrary God loves to 'fill the hungry with good things,' (Luke 1:53). In fact His invitation in both Old and New Testaments is to come thirsty and hungry for *more*, to 'Come, buy wine and milk without money and without cost.' (Isaiah 55:1). Then there is David's testimony, because the Lord is my Shepherd 'I shall not be in want' (Psalm 23:1), which encourages us even further that, not only do we have a heavenly Father who is rich in all the things that I need, but that I also have a Shepherd who is delighted to lead me and supply all those things.

The Lord doesn't mind us feeling hungry for more, in fact He loves it. From His own mouth we hear Him say, 'Blessed are those who hunger and thirst for righteousness for they will be *filled*.' (Matthew 5:6). And let's not forget that the Laodicean church was rebuked for claiming, "I am rich; I have acquired wealth and do not need a thing", not realising that spiritually they were 'wretched, pitiful, poor, blind and naked'. (Revelation 3:17). The fact is that I am in a good place when I feel my 'lack' or 'poverty' in an area, because whatever I need *'more of',* the Lord has it, and provided that it is in His will for me, He will give it and give it freely. His purpose and plan for us is that we should find *'fullness'* and that until we have reached that place, we can always be asking for *'more'*.

We can ask for **more** forgiveness, and **more** of His righteousness. 'If we confess our sins, He is faithful and just to forgive us our sins and cleanse us from **all** unrighteousness.' (1 John 1:9, AV) We can ask for **more** of His life to flow into us, 'I will give unto him that is athirst of the fountain of the water of life **freely**.' (Revelation 21:6, AV). And 'whosoever will, let him take of the water of life **freely**'. (Revelation 22:17, AV). And what about His wisdom and guidance? 'If any of you lacks wisdom, he should ask of God, who **gives generously** to all without finding fault, and it will be given him.' (James 1:5). 'He who did not spare His own Son, but delivered Him over for us all, how will He not also with Him **freely give** us all things?' (Romans 8:32, NASB). In fact whatever we need in order to grow spiritually, is already ours for the asking, 'in Christ'.

We have a generous and giving God, whose heart's desire is that we should receive in **full measure** all the riches that Jesus paid for on the cross; every blessing pertaining to our New Life in Christ, (See 2 Peter 1:3). God's desire is that we, Christ's body on earth, should be **'the fullness of Him who fills everything in every way.'** (Ephesians 1:23), and that we might know the height, breadth, length and depth of the love of Christ that passes knowledge, in order **'that you may be filled up with all the fullness of God.'** (Ephesians 3:19, NASB). And the reason that God gave the ministry gifts of apostles, prophets, evangelists, pastors and teachers, was in order that we might attain to **'the whole measure of the fullness of Christ'**. (Ephesians 4:13).

Activation . . .

Today give thanks when you become aware of a lack in any area. That feeling 'hungry' is the pre-emptor to being *filled*. When you feel that you are lacking in faith, love, or patience etc, turn to the Lord and say "thank you Lord that you have allowed me to recognise my poverty in this area, that you have stirred my hunger, and that you are wanting to *fill* me to overflowing by your Spirit." Then let that thankfulness position you to receive all that your loving and generous Father wants to pour into your life. Have confidence today that He will always respond when you, like Oliver say, "Please Lord, can I have some *more*".

DAY 279 | Thanksgiving for God's Extravagance

Extravagant ... meaning — Immoderate; exceeding the bounds of reason; profuse, wasteful; exorbitant. [Oxford Dictionary].

When I was a child, being a post war baby, I learnt that being 'extravagant' was not a virtue. Whether you were extravagant with the amount of sugar you put in a drink, the amount of money you spent on clothes, or the amount of time you wasted, an extravagant lifestyle was not to be admired. The only time extravagance was allowed was when it involved a present. Extravagance then denoted, not just your wealth, but also the value you placed on the recipient of your gift, and so I feel that this aspect of God definitely needs further exploration; I am talking about His willingness to be extravagant, to give us 'more' than we need.

We can see the extravagance of our omnipotent God in so many aspects of creation all around us. We see extravagance, over and above that which is necessary for life to exists: In the billions and billions of stars that are never seen, and the millions of desert and Alpine meadow flowers that live and die unappreciated. And we see God's extravagance supremely displayed in all the acts of love, about which we read in the gospels. These stories give us a unique glimpse into the extravagant heart of our God towards humankind, the crown of His extravagant creation. There is 'no expense spared' when the Lord moves to meet the needs of those who call on Him.

Let's take a look at the wedding in Cana of Galilee where, in response to the problem of a shortage of wine, (which could have caused a huge amount of shame), Jesus creates something in the order of 120 gallons of the best wine. (John 2:1-10). In response to a hungry crowd, without sustenance and far from home, He provides a meal for five thousand plus people with surplus enough to fill twelve baskets. (Luke 9:10-17). An extravagance then repeated with four thousand people. (Mark 8:1-8). (Just in case they missed it the first time!!). Then when the fishermen are struggling for a catch, He guides them to where they should fish and suddenly, 'they were unable to haul in the net because of the large number of fish.' (John 21:6. See also Luke 5:5-7, where the boats were so full they began to sink).

We also learn about God's extravagance in the language used in the Bible that reveals the explosively generous heart of God towards His family. To start with God **loved us so much that He gave His only Son to die for us** in order that we might become His children. That is just incredible generosity! The Apostle John reiterates this, writing '**How great is the love the Father has lavished on us, that we should be called children of God**'. (1 John 3:1). This extravagant level of generosity is largely incomprehensible to us. It's Immoderate, exceeding the bounds of reason? (See the definition above). There is nothing begrudging about God, and that truth alone should release our faith.

Paul had such a grasp of the magnitude of God's love that he wrote that not only is this a love that passes knowledge; unfathomable in its height, length, depth and breadth, but that this God of ours 'is able to do **exceedingly abundantly above all that we ask or think** according to the power that worketh in us.' (Ephesians 3:20, AV). Now that is some love and power that He has put to work in our lives. He will therefore withhold nothing from us that will bring the fulfillment of His purposes to make us like Jesus, to conform us to the image of His Son. (See Romans 8:29). In fact 'His divine power has given us everything we need for life and Godliness...' (2 peter 1:3).

These scriptures show us that our extravagant God does indeed have great wealth, and that He also puts great value on us His children. Our thanksgiving to the Lord for His open and generous heart towards us will, I believe, break us free from any poverty mentality we may have, when it comes to the resources that are ours in Christ by the Holy Spirit's power. Resources that are freely given to us by the Lord to work in us 'both to will **and to do** for His good pleasure.' (Philippians 2:13, NASB).

Activation...

Today release to God your thanksgiving that He is beyond generous, and that He values you highly. It's not that there will only be just enough, He is willing to pour into you over and above anything you can ask or even think. (Ephesians 3:20).

DAY 280 | Thanksgiving for every Fresh Challenge

Sometimes our very extravagant God needs to provoke us with fresh challenges in order that we will pull on Him for all the blessings and resources that He has for us. As we mentioned before, He loves to fill the hungry with good things, and there is nothing like a new situation to provoke that hunger in us for **more**.

We can probably all recognise that we grow the most when we are faced with a new challenge. We grow in those times when we feel that our own resources are not enough and that we are being 'stretched'. In those times we can go one of two ways. We can either call on the Lord for more grace, or call on Him to remove the challenge, and remove us from the situation. So often we would prefer the latter, but our extremely loving and extravagant heavenly Father often prefers the first. He would rather 'grow us' than just 'rescue us'.

In the world of sport and athletics a good coach will train a sports person with an eye to building up stamina and skill, and very often the best way to improve in an area of sport is by playing against a better player. The challenge of that experience often draws out the very best in the one being trained. A good coach will therefore keep the challenge to a level where the trainee is not overwhelmed but is stretched and developed.

Our God is like a good coach, and in His care for us He is not going to give us more than we can manage. His purposes and plans are to grow us, not to sink us, but very often we have less confidence in ourselves, or in 'Christ in us', than God Himself has. For example Paul writing about the challenge of resisting temptation says that, not only is it common to all men, but that 'He will not let you be tempted beyond what you can bear. But when you are tempted, He will also provide a way out so that you can stand up under it.' (1 Corinthians 10:13). And the same principle applies I believe to other kinds of challenge too.

In whatever form the challenge comes, let us thank the Lord for it. This will increase our faith that the Lord believes in us, and believes in all the resources that we have in Christ through the indwelling Holy Spirit. He is our friend, our helper, our coach and our champion. He is with us to grow us and to help us succeed. He wants us to get to that place where we can say with Paul, "I can do everything through Him who gives me strength." (Philippians 4:13). Therefore I believe the Lord would love for us to get excited about every fresh challenge.

The second reason why we need to give thanks in the face of difficulty and challenge is that our wonderful heavenly Father will catch us if we fail and need to 're-group' in order to try again and grow some more. The good news is that, like the mother eagle, He will be ready to catch us if our 'flapping around' doesn't result in a smooth flight. This is the back story to the wonderful scripture in Deuteronomy 32:10,11 where, referring to the people of God and their relationship with Him, the writer says 'He (God) shielded him (His people Israel) and cared for him: He guarded him as the apple of His eye, like an eagle that stirs up its nest and hovers over its young, that spreads its wings to catch them and carries them on its pinions.'

Our Heavenly Father always has plans to mature us and increase our spiritual stature and sometimes, like the mother eagle, He has to destroy the nest – our safe place – in order to get us to fly. The mother eagle will carry the young bird that has failed to fly, on her wings back to whatever is left of the nest. She will then encourage the young bird to keep trying until those wing muscles are strong enough to carry the young bird itself. And so for us, as life throws up fresh challenges, we can be sure that the Lord is shielding us, caring for us and ready to catch us if we fall or are struggling to meet the challenge before us.

Activation ...

So today there are two good reasons to give thanks to God when you are facing difficult or challenging circumstances. Thank Him that He thinks you are ready to grow in a particular area of your life as you draw on all the grace that comes with His empowering presence, that is now **yours** since you are 'in Christ'. And then you can thank Him that 'if at first you don't succeed', He will be there, hovering over you, ready to catch you and restore you until you are ready to 'go again'!

DAY 281 | Thanksgiving that Slows me Down!

"Slow me down?" I hear you say, "I need something to speed me up, there always seems so much to do. I'm constantly trying to fit a quart into a pint pot." Perhaps that has always been part of modern life but I think that because of the increased use of our phones, ipads, zoom, twitter, facebook and Netflix etc, the enemy has made sure that our minds and emotions stay busy, full and preoccupied, so that we are hurrying physically, mentally and emotionally, from one thing to the next. It's called 'Hurry Sickness'.

I am writing this because I heard recently of a book by John Mark Comer called 'The Ruthless Elimination of Hurry' published by Hodder and Stoughton in 2019.[1] Its title reflects a comment from the late Dallas Willard who, in answer to the question, "What do I need to do to become the person I want to be?" replied, "Ruthlessly eliminate hurry from your life." And when asked what else? He replied "There is nothing else, hurry is the great enemy of spiritual life in our day". Wow!

Other big names have also identified hurry as a problem. The Psychologist Carl Jung is quoted as saying, "Hurry is not of the devil, it is the devil."[2] Corrie Ten Boom said something similar, "If the devil can't make you sin, he'll make you busy."[3] And we, in this digital age, have to square up to the fact that even if we control our diaries, our business so often comes through the alert on the phone that we **have** to look at, the Netflix binge, the addiction to seeing what's happening in other lives through face-book, and perhaps the overarching ethos that texts, emails, twitter etc., have to be responded to in the moment, regardless of what we are doing, or who we are with, including our one-on-one time with the Lord.

Now we have written before about how thanksgiving helps us to relish and savour each moment; about how thanksgiving slows us down on our walks (or even on a drive) to enjoy the wonders of creation, the changing seasons, the magnificence of the sky, day or night. Thanksgiving can help to keep us 'in the moment' as we become grateful and aware of the preciousness of time spent with individual people in different scenarios, and in different places. But now I can see that it is also a weapon that can help us to fight the 'Hurry Sickness' in the world around us, and maybe in our own inner world.

This 'hurry sickness' can start with just a thought. I wonder how many times you hear yourself say "I have to do this". "I must go here", "I ought to respond immediately to that", "I should see this". "I need to ... straight away." It can feel like there is an urgency to absolutely everything we touch these days, and sometimes there is of course – but really everything?? We used to talk about how the urgent can easily crowd out the important. We used to suggest to people that answer phones were the way to ensure that they had a Sabbath rest day. Since mobile phones have arrived however, it's now more a case of turning the phone off, or removing it to another space, as the urgency of responding to an alert distracts us from the important thing that we are doing.

I believe, and I am working hard at this myself, that to respond to people and to situations that command our attention 'with thanksgiving' is a powerful antidote to being 'driven'. This is because when we thank the Lord for whatever it is that is drawing our attention, we immediately engage with Him, and so the Holy Spirit can help us to discern what it is good and right to do, **or not to do**, in response. Thanksgiving – for the person, the event, the decision, the request, the thing that threatens to fill and preoccupy our mind – is like pressing the pause button, giving us time to think before we respond, and time to listen for the Lord's wisdom and leading.

Activation ...

As you read through the gospels, you will see Jesus, walking through life with grace and dignity, knowing when to withdraw and talk to His Father, (Luke 5:15,16), when to respond and allow an interruption, (Luke 8:42-48), when to ignore and avoid a situation, (Luke 4:28-30), and when to spend special time with His friends. (Luke 9:28-36). So in these days use this wonderful gift of thanksgiving as part of your weaponry in the fight to eliminate hurry from your life. Use thanksgiving to keep your connection with Father, Son and Holy Spirit strong and clear, as you respond to Jesus' invitation, "Walk with me and work with Me – watch how I do it. Learn (from Me) the unforced rhythms of grace." (Matthew 11:28, The Message).

DAY 282 | Thanksgiving that Defuses a Culture of Entitlement

It seems to me that one of snares of 21st century living is the increase around us, and sometimes in us, of a culture of entitlement. Of course this has always been there in human nature. As a child you get a wonderful present at Christmas from an aunt, or a grandparent, and you are thrilled and grateful. It's a beautiful gift. Next year another comes and again you are thrilled and grateful. And so it goes on for several years and soon you are not just looking forward happily to the gift at Christmas but you are expecting it. Then one Christmas comes and there is just a small gift and, instead of being grateful, you are disappointed. This is natural, but your mood can dip further. The gift was expected and you felt entitled to a good gift from that Aunt and now you are miserable, maybe even a little cross.

Back in 1948, after the war, I think many people were thrilled with the gift of free health care in the new NHS and the increasing availability of butter, meat and sugar etc. Many years on we can feel entitled to these things as our right, and gratitude can slip away and be replaced by something much less healthy for our souls, emotions and spirits. We can feel entitled to a centrally heated house, a good balanced diet, a wide variety of food in the shops, public services that provide for our needs, and much more. Yet many in our world don't have these 'necessities'.

In the 1970's Mark, my husband, worked for a year in Uganda as a doctor. Idi Amin was in power. There were many shortages. What they could offer people was very limited, but it was better than nothing. What he noticed was how grateful many people were. Back in England, there was so much more in the way of services, equipment and medicine available in the NHS, but people were not always that grateful. Sometimes those with little are more grateful than those with much.

Has high expectation developed into a sort of entitlement and too much emphasis on 'my rights'? Has high expectation tarnished, or even soured the hearts and minds of some of us resulting in a loss of gratitude and thankfulness? Even more troubling can be a loss of gratitude and thankfulness, coupled with a strong sense of expectation, and 'my rights,' lead me towards feeling a victim of others, the system, or circumstances. Worse still, could I end up feeling a victim of God? "He hasn't done what He ought to have done." I wonder if Job felt a little of that?

It is great that we have 'rights' that we can and do exercise, such as access to health care, a pension when we reach a certain age, freedom from accepting bullying or abuse in life, and much more. And it is good to see these benefits extended to more people across the globe. But in the spirit of Proverbs 4:23 'Above all else, guard your heart, for it is the wellspring of life.' it is important that our rights and privileges do not prevent us from having a heart bursting with thankfulness and gratitude for all the goodness, kindness and mercy of God to me daily. It may be 'my right' to have free treatment on the NHS. But let me not fail to be filled with gratitude and thanksgiving to God that I have received that major blessing to my health and well being.

Jeremiah was a servant of God who felt that God had let Him down in a big way. His lament/complaint is recorded for us in Lamentation 3:1-19. Surely he, who had been doing God's work had a 'right' to be looked after by God. He then 'calls to mind' God's great love and mercy. He remembers that it is 'because of the Lord's great love we are not consumed for His compassions never fail. They are new every morning; great is your faithfulness.' (verse 21-24). We are not specifically told that He gave thanks for that love, but somehow remembering God's love and faithfulness with gratitude worked for him. He gains fresh hope and can declare, 'the Lord is good to those whose hope is in him.'(verse 25).

Activation ...

If the saying that 'my attitude affects the altitude at which I fly in life' is true then I think an 'attitude of gratitude' manifested in a life of thanksgiving is likely to make me a high flyer! So don't forget to express lots of gratitude to God when you receive things, especially those things to which you feel you have a right. This will bless the Lord and will keep you in a place of 'walking humbly with your God.' (Micah 6:8). Let gratitude and thanksgiving be like powerful cleansing, health giving streams and rivers washing out any of that threatening poison of 'entitlement' from my heart, mind and attitudes.

DAY 283 | Gratitude and my Complaint!

We wrote yesterday about the need to avoid letting a spirit of entitlement sour our relationship with the Lord. So where does staying in 'faith' sit between confidence in the Lord's extravagant provision for us, and entitlement. Well I think that 'faith' slips over into entitlement when we find ourselves harbouring disappointment and saying something like, "I thought the Lord was going to ...", or "Lord, why didn't you ... ?" or even "I don't understand, if the Lord loves me, (sister 'A', or brother 'B'), why did He let that happen?" Faith can slip into entitlement when our hoped for expectations are dashed, and this is when our disappointment can turn into disillusionment.

Jeremiah is someone who certainly, and understandably, felt that God had let Him down in a big way. His lament/complaint is recorded for us in Lamentation. Have a read of chapter 3:1-19. Surely he, who had been doing God's work, had a 'right' to be looked after by God. His disillusionment took him to the place where he didn't just feel let down by God, but positively persecuted. He even wrote things like ... 'He has walled me in so I cannot escape; he has weighed me down with chains. Even when I call out or cry for help, he shuts out my prayer.' 'He pierced my heart with arrows from His quiver.' Jeremiah was not a happy man!

The good news was that he took his complaint to God, and we hear the dialogue between them in Jeremiah 15: 15-21. In answer to his questions, 'Why is my pain unending and my wound grievous and incurable? Will you be to me like a deceptive brook, like a spring that fails?' (i.e like something that promises a great deal but doesn't deliver?), the Lord has this to say ... (and this needs to be read in an older version, or the Amplified Bible, to get the full weight of it.)

"If you return, (and give up this mistaken tone of distrust and despair), then I will give you again a settled place of quiet *and* safety, and you will be My minister; and if you **separate the precious from the vile [cleansing your own heart from unworthy and unwarranted suspicions concerning God's faithfulness]**, you shall be my mouthpiece ... And I will make you a fortified, bronze wall ... for I am with you to save *and* deliver you, says the Lord.'

So how does Jeremiah do that? How does he separate the precious (his faith) from the vile, (his doubts)? Well yesterday we noted that Jeremiah was able to do that as he, 'calls to mind' God's great and steadfast love and his mercy; that it is 'Because of the Lord's great love that we are not consumed.'

Many years ago now I was moved by a friend who, going through a very difficult and protracted time with her family, seemed to be very steady in her faith. When we asked further about how she was managing to 'stay in faith', she quoted those words, "It is because of the Lord's mercy that we are not consumed". In other words, He has died for us and saved us. If we actually got what we deserved we would all be consumed. I'm not **entitled** to anything more. Salvation itself, all it means, and all it has achieved for me for all eternity, is so big, so immense, why should I complain if the other things that I would want at this time seem to be lacking?

When I am feeling disappointed, and it seems that, in spite of God's declared character and promises, I am feeling that He hasn't 'come through' for me, I really, really need to guard my heart with thanksgiving. I need to remind myself with thanksgiving of all that He **has** done. I need to look at the cross again and thank Him for my salvation. I need to remember the wonderful truth of 'Emmanuel' – God is with me, and 'Christ in you, the hope of Glory.' (Colossians 1:27). I need to call to mind my history, my journey, my testimony and give thanks for all the ways in which He has been there for me in the past.

Activation . . .

Always let thanksgiving keep you 'in faith' for more of God's goodness. It will help in a way that complaints won't. Thanksgiving will keep you in those moments when, like Basilea Schlink, you need to say, "My Father I don't understand you but I do trust you." Or even to declare like Job, "Though He slay me, yet will I hope in Him; . . ." (Job 13:15), and "I know *that* my redeemer liveth, and *that* he shall stand in the latter *day* upon the earth: And *though* worms destroy this *body*, yet in my flesh shall I see God:" (Job 19:25,26, AV). Now that's the kind of faith that is precious to God!

DAY 284 | Thanksgiving and Delay

One of the things that might confuse us in our walk with the Lord is the mystery of God's timings. They are often so very different from ours. That is probably not really surprising, given that He lives in eternity and we in finite time. His perspective must necessarily be very different to ours because, unlike God, we live in this world and our physical life will one day end. Death is the only certainty that we have in life right from the day we are born.

Apart from this truth of our lives being of limited duration, we also now live in a culture of 'immediate' and 'instant'!! Several hundreds of years ago, life in a rural community would have been governed by the seasons and by the rhythms of the sun and moon. Now in our digital age, we increasingly live driven by the demand for 24/7 responses in all kinds of areas of life. It's no longer just that we have instant coffee and instant food, now big things like the fortunes of individuals, companies and even nations can be altered in a few minutes on the stock exchange or by a lottery win.

News of events circle the globe in a few minutes throughout the day and the night, and a text, an email, or a social media post can alter someone's life in a moment, for better or for worse. And so in our own lives, responding to and keeping up with the speed of everyday life, can make us impatient and irritated with unexpected delays of any kind, and we can easily find ourselves putting our time frames onto God which can complicate our relationship with Him.

God's promises are not time limited, or time sensitive like so many offers that are thrust into our consciousness in these days. God does things in His way and in His time, not mine. We just have to look at the life of a man like Joseph, to see a huge time lapse between the prophetic dreams that he had as a young man of seventeen in Canaan and the fulfillment of that dream in Egypt some thirteen years later when he was thirty. (See Genesis 37-41).

Moses understood this. He was a man who had to wait forty years for the restoration that he needed, in order for him to fulfil his destiny and lead his people. In his prayer recorded for us in Psalm 90:4 he says, **'a thousand**

years in your sight are like a day that has just gone by, or like a watch in the night.' Then there is David who had to wait many years (a good deal of it as an outlaw) for the fulfilment of God's words to him through Samuel's declaration and anointing of him as king. He later wrote 'But I trust in you, O Lord; I say "You are my God." **My times are in your hands**; deliver me from my enemies and from those who pursue me. Let your face shine on your servant; save me in your unfailing love.' (Psalm 31:15,16). He had grasped that God's timings are different to ours, and also that the wait might not be in comfortable circumstances.

So what of us? If these towering figures of the Old Testament had to 'wait' in very difficult circumstances for the Lord to show Himself faithful to His words, perhaps we shouldn't be surprised that, with God, answers come but often seem to us to be unnecessarily delayed. It can sometimes feel 'too late' as for Sarah and Abraham. (See Genesis 18:10-15), but we are told in Hebrews 6:12 to 'imitate those who through faith and patience inherit what has been promised.' 'Faith and patience'! An interesting combination. Shouldn't real faith bring an instant answer??

Paul after teaching the saints about the whole armour of God finishes by encouraging them to be persevering in their prayers for each other saying, 'With all prayer and petition pray at all times in the Spirit, and with this in view, be on the alert with all **perseverance** and petition for all the saints,' (Ephesians 6:18, NASB). I think he is telling us that spiritual battles take time, but that as they do, and if we are in the right place with God, and have the right attitude, we will grow and mature.

Activation ...

Is there delay in some aspect of your life about which you have been praying, or in the answer to your prayers for another? Remember that God stands outside of time and so like David intentionally give thanks as you pray and declare to the Lord **'my times are in your hand.'**

DAY 285 | Thanksgiving and Persevering in Faith

It can be particularly challenging to wait for the Lord's timings when we are in trouble and the Lord seems to have forgotten us. Looking at the prophet Jeremiah, who was suffering because of his calling to bring God's word to the people of Israel, we can see that the main focus of the enemy's attack on Jeremiah was to cast doubt on the character and the goodness of God. This attack on Jeremiah's faith, was fundamental to his good relationship with God, and his ministry as God's prophet to the nation of Israel. The devil has used that same trick over and over again, sometimes sadly to great effect.

It started with Eve when the serpent first of all says. "Did God really say, 'You must not eat from any tree in the garden'?" (Genesis 3:1-6), throwing doubt into her mind about what God had said. Then having done that he goes on to blatantly contradict God, "You will not surely die," (This was a clever half truth because they didn't die physically straight away. Death was first of all spiritual then physical.) And finally, the trump card, an insinuation that God is mean and just keeping them down. He says, "For God knows that when you eat of it your eyes will be opened, and you will be like God, knowing good and evil." By saying that, he also gave a significant boost to the appetising nature of the fruit, by attributing to it the ability to give wisdom to the one who consumed it. Wow! That is clever.

I think that often when we find ourselves harbouring a 'complaint' against God, and what He is (or isn't) doing for us, or if we are just simply confused about how life is going, the enemy is right there ready with his lies, half truths, and insinuations and, if we are not careful, our befuddled minds will take his thoughts on board, especially if they resonate with what we are already feeling or thinking. At these times thanksgiving and gratitude can powerfully help to guard our hearts and minds by keeping us focused on the truth of 'who God is' and 'what He is like'.

When we are in trouble and God seems far away, it's like being at a cross roads. To the left I can go down the road labeled, 'God isn't as good and kind as He says He is'. To the right I can go down the road labeled, 'There is something wrong with me since God is not bothered with for me.' Both of those roads (replace my words with your own version of both), lead us away from God and down a spiritual cul-de-sac. The road ahead however is labelled, 'I may not understand, but God is good, He loves me, and I am going to press into Him for grace to walk with Him through this season.'

That road straight ahead involves embracing 'mystery'; the mystery of God's timings on things, of His higher purposes that I often, in the moment, don't 'get'. The mystery that we are caught in a battle between two world systems, the kingdom of light and the kingdom of darkness, a battle of which we only catch glimpses in scripture, (see Daniel 10:12-14). The mystery that my faith actually grows, and I mature spiritually in times of trouble. And finally the mystery that God is working in us for good in the light of eternity, and not just for our comfort in this life.

Jeremiah found peace and hope again when he, 'called to mind' God's great and steadfast love and his mercy. When he remembered that it was, 'Because of the Lord's great love that we are not consumed, for his compassions never fail.' (Lamentations 3:21-22). So when we are in those situations where God seems to be silent, or when things seem to be going badly for us and He doesn't immediately come to our rescue; when the promises that we have read in His Word seem remote and unlikely to be fulfilled, and in times when we are vulnerable; at these times our thanksgiving really, really matters. These are the 1 Thessalonians 5:18 times when we need to offer up our sacrifice of praise, and give thanks. (See also Hebrews 13:15, NASB and Psalm 50:14, NASB).

Activation ...

In your seasons of perplexity refuse to go to the path on the right – doubting God's goodness and love, or to the left – deciding it must be your fault, and instead go straight ahead with thanksgiving. Fill your heart with thanksgiving and prevent it from becoming fertile ground for the seeds of discontent which lead to doubt and then fear. Giving thanks at these times will help you to set your face to walk down that central road. There will be light on your path there, because it's the road of which Isaiah spoke, 'Come, O house of Jacob, let us walk in the light of the Lord.' (Isaiah 2:5).

DAY 286 | Thanksgiving and the Trojan Horse Effect

We are probably all familiar with the story of the Trojan Horse, and how the Greek soldiers used it to enter the city of Troy and win the Trojan war. It is now often used as a metaphor for getting yourself, someone else, or your ideas inside an enemy fortress, or domain, in order to 'win' a victory. It occurred to me this morning that we – God's people – are like His Trojan horse, bringing His Kingdom into a dark world that doesn't, at the moment, recognise His Kingship. As we look around us and read the news, and see anti-Christian groups become more and more vocal in today's post Christian society, we can begin to feel outnumbered and a bit beleaguered, but our God still has a plan and it involves you and me!!

The prophet Habakkuk writing at a time when God's people were far from Him and under His judgment, made an incredible declaration. You may have heard it quoted, 'For the earth will be filled with the knowledge of the glory of the Lord as the waters cover the sea." (Habakkuk 2:14). In these days I think that many of us are praying to see the 'knowledge of the glory of God' fill the earth and push back the darkness. So how can the story of the Trojan Horse help to increase our faith?

Well I think it is like this; we live on earth, like everybody else, but unlike others all around us we carry God's presence in the same way as that Trojan horse carried in the Greek soldiers. This is because 'our citizenship is in heaven.' (Philippians 3:20) and God's plan is to bring His Kingdom into this world through us. Christ lives in us and so we carry His glory, (John 17:22), and we are charged with the task of spreading His glory throughout the earth.

When Jesus was presented as a baby at the Temple, Simeon prophetically declared Him to be, 'a light for revelation to the gentiles and for glory to your people Israel'. (Luke2:32). Jesus later told His followers not just that He was the Light of the world, but "You are the light of the world," and He told them not to hide that light but to "let your light shine before men, that they may see your good deeds and praise your Father in Heaven". (Matthew 5:14-16). Amazing as it might seem, I believe that 'the knowledge of the

Glory of God,' is going to spread through the earth, as we carry it into the darkest places because that same Glory rests upon us, His people.

So how can we do that? How can we be sure that we are an 'effective Trojan horse' carrying the 'light of God' and the 'might of God's Kingdom' as an invading, liberating presence into our present dark world? I believe there are two things that will significantly help us in this matter. Firstly we need to recognise who we are in the 'spirit' world, and what we carry, and then we need to learn how to intentionally release the river of life that flows through us into the world around us. (More of that tomorrow).

We need to know that we don't have to be in a worship meeting, or a bible week, or a conference with thousands of others, to be effective. Psalm 34:5 tells us that, 'those who look to him are radiant; their faces are never covered with shame.' Thanksgiving in any situation, any scenario and any place, turns my gaze upon Him, thanksgiving causes me to 'look at Him' and away from me, from my ability, talents, performance and yes even from how well I am 'shining' for Jesus. And as I look to Him with worship and thanksgiving in my heart, I will shine. It's just a spiritual fact.

We heard recently of a converted warlock who explained that, before his conversion, he could always identify Christians, because there was 'light' coming from them. Often, I think, people of the darkness see what we can't. Maybe that is why so many medieval paintings depict the saints with light around their heads, their 'halo'. This then is about 'who we now are in Christ', and that He is in me. The more I recognise who I now am, and what I am carrying of His presence and glory, the more likely I am to shine and walk as He would walk. (See 1 John 2:6).

Activation ...

Matthew, quoting from the prophet Isaiah wrote, "the people living in darkness have seen a great light; on those living in the land of the shadow of death a light has dawned." (Matthew 4:16). So today keep looking to Jesus and stay radiant as you give thanks in all things, and at all times, for who you now are in Christ, and for the truth that you are included in His plans to invade the darkness of this world and fill it with the light of the knowledge of His Glory.

DAY 287 | Thanksgiving and Releasing the Glory of God

In Isaiah 60:1-3, we read the exhortation, given to the nation of Israel long ago, and recorded here for us today. 'ARISE, SHINE, for your light has come, and the glory of the Lord rises upon you. See, darkness covers the earth and thick darkness the peoples, but the Lord rises upon you and His glory appears over you. Nations will come to your light and kings to the brightness of your rising.' We wrote yesterday how we, as citizens of heaven, are God's 'Trojan Horse' because we carry His glory, His Kingdom, into this world and into the kingdom of darkness. We said that understanding who we are spiritually, and what we carry, was of utmost importance if we are to recognise our part in the fulfillment of the prophesy that 'the earth will be filled with the knowledge of the glory of God as the waters cover the sea'.

We noted that the key to 'shining' our light was in giving thanks for our new identity, and the reality that we carry God's glory in the earth. This helps us to keep our eyes on Him, and not on ourselves. Remember Psalm 34:5 tells us that if we can keep our eyes on Him, we will be radiant. So today we are looking at how thanksgiving also plays a key role as we seek to intentionally and prophetically release the blessings of heaven through our words, actions and prayers into the darkness of this world.

Firstly 'Thank You' helps me to connect with the Lord in 'the moment' and at any moment, enabling me to remember and therefore receive all His promises for the challenges that each moment brings. It reminds me of who I now am in this world. It also opens my eyes to the Lord's presence, and all the provision that His presence with, and in, me carries. It lifts my gaze to heaven's resources and God's heart of love, enabling me to rise up in faith and claim those same promises, as well as the prophetic words that have been spoken over me.

Secondly 'Thank You' helps me to listen with my spirit to the promptings of the Lord, not those of my old self or the enemy. 'Thank You' destroys any negativity, doubt, fear or unbelief, by blocking the enemy's voice. It fills me with faith and thereby stops doubts from hindering me as I seek to speak and act in response to the promptings of the Holy Spirit.

Thirdly 'Thank You' releases the Holy Spirit to fill me with wisdom, hope, joy and expectancy which in turn gives me the boldness and confidence to step out in faith and declare what I have heard from the heart of God; to release the blessings that He has for the one whom I am with, or the situation in which I am standing. Simply put 'Thank you', from my heart, positions me to prophecy through the spoken word, or through my actions and prayers.

I could go on and I hope you will build your own list, but simply put, thank you allows that river of life to keep flowing through me in all and any situation, and as the Spirit flows, so the 'fruit of the Spirit' grows in me, and that helps me to obey Isaiah 60:1; to 'Arise and Shine' spiritually speaking. And the wonderful thing is *I can do it*! I can give thanks anywhere and at any time of the day or night.

Wherever we are, in a hospital bed, a pub, a school, our home, the shops, the hairdresser, the office, or the football game, we are the closest some people will get to touching the life of God. (See Matthew 10:7 and Luke 10:9). It's our privilege and honour to represent the King and release the blessings, the very life of God, that we carry as His children, into any and every situation in which we find ourselves.

Activation . . .

A prayer for today. "Lord I am so grateful that 'Thank You' helps me to connect with you 'in the moment', that it lifts my gaze to heaven and opens my eyes to your presence Lord, and all the provision and resources in your heart of love. It is so wonderful that my 'Thank You' releases the Holy Spirit, allowing Him to fill me with hope, joy and expectancy. Help me to listen with my spirit to your promptings Lord. And I ask today that you will use me to release some more of your glory into this world through my words, my actions and my prayers. May your kingdom come and your will be done, on earth where I am, as it is in heaven. For it is Your Kingdom, Your Power and Your Glory for ever and ever Amen."

DAY 288 | Thanksgiving and Courage

One of the ways in which we can 'shine' in these shaking times is by letting the Lord deal with our anxieties so that we are free of them. When Jesus was on earth He spoke about the signs that would herald the coming of His Kingdom. He talks of signs in the heavens, of 'dismay among the nations', perplexity at the roaring of the seas and men 'fainting from fear', at the expectation of things that were coming upon the world. (Luke 21:25,26).

We know that the end of the ages is going to be marked by shaking times. (See Matthew 24:36-42). How near we are to those days no one knows but we are certainly living in times in which, all over the world, there are problems arising which mankind seems unable or unwilling to 'fix'. In our own country anxiety levels, (and what is anxiety but another name for fear?) are on the rise; and this inspite of all kinds of advice, counselling techniques and quasi religious means to combat anxiety and keep everyone in 'peace'.

So if fear (or anxiety) is on the rise and if it is something which many seem unable to contain or combat, then we God's people can, by listening to our heavenly Father, gain our own victory over anxiety. We can thereby demonstrate to the world that our God is good, powerful, mighty and present with us in all our troubles. We will be able to 'shine' as we declare with the Psalmist, **'God is our refuge and strength, an ever-present help in trouble, therefore we will not fear, though the earth give way, and the mountains fall into the heart of the sea, though its waters roar and foam and the mountains quake with their surging.'** (Psalm 46:1-3).

And what about David's declaration in Psalm 23, **'Even though I walk through the valley of the shadow of death, I will fear no evil, for you are with me.'** Or from The Passion Translation 'Lord, even when your path takes me through the valley of deepest darkness, **fear will never conquer me, for you already have.'** These verses of course follow the earlier ones where David is recalling that the Lord has shepherded him through many different seasons in his life. In other words his bold declaration that he will not fear any evil is based on his recalling of God's faithfulness to him in times past.

David wasn't afraid of Goliath, for example, because of his previous experiences with wild animals. "The Lord who delivered me from the paw of the lion and the paw of the bear will deliver me from the hand of the Philistine" (1 Samuel 17: 34-37). John Newton expressed something similar in his wonderful hymn as he reminds us of the power of reviewing the times in our lives when the Lord has helped us . . . **'His love in times past, forbids me to think, He'll leave me at last in trouble to sink, each sweet Ebenezer I have in review, confirms His good pleasure, to help me quite through.'** Ebenezer means 'stone of help' and when the prophet Samuel set it up he declared, "Thus far the Lord has helped us" (1 Samuel 7:12).

If remembering all that the Lord has done for me will help me to overcome anxiety in the 'now', then we need to recognise again that 'Thanksgiving' is one of the best ways to remember and recount all that the Lord has done for me? Why? Because it is very hard to be thanking God for all He has done for me and not to find my hope and faith in His love and power for today's issues growing. And it is so practical. As I bring things to mind and thank God for His love, kindness, goodness and answers, in all sorts of real life situations that I have faced, faith for today and tomorrow rises. Confidence and courage grow even in the face of anxiety provoking situations.

David's active, intentional, focused remembering fuelled his faith and gave him the confidence to go where no one else dared, as He trusted His God. So we need to get talking to ourselves. If faith comes by hearing (Romans 10:17), then my ears and heart need to hear me remembering and then recounting all that God has done for me, from the huge to the apparently trivial, (although in actual fact nothing God does is trivial.)

Activation . . .

Use the power of thanksgiving today whenever you need to battle fears or anxieties. Strengthen yourself and take hold of the courage that giving thanks and remembering God's past deliverances brings to your heart. Read through Psalm 107 or Psalm 136 and see how good this practice of thanksgiving for 'past deliverances' can be.

DAY 289 | Thanksgiving and Growth

Walking in our nearby wood this morning I became aware of many, many small oak tree saplings. They varied in height and some were barely waist high. Then I looked up to see the full height of the oak trees that had shed their acorns to enable this vast little army of oaks to take root and to grow, and the whole mystery of 'growth' took hold of me.

Every plant, tree and flower that God has created, and indeed everything in the animal kingdom too, starts off as a tiny seed, a small kernel or nut, and grows and grows and grows until it can be seen in all its magnificence. Now to state the obvious, that just doesn't happen with 'man made' things. 'Man made' things start life in their completed form and then tend to decay, wear out, break down, and need renovation.

Inbuilt growth and cell renewal is the prerogative of the things that our creator God makes, and that renewal and growth happens year after year because of the life that the Lord has put in all things natural, provided that it is not destroyed by man's interventions.

I found great encouragement in pondering over these things, because as can happen to all of us, events can unfold that make us feel that we have failed in some way to live and be the 'New Person in Christ' about which we were sharing in Book Three. There are those times when far from feeling like 'an oak of righteousness', (Isaiah 61:3), we can feel like one of those very small saplings that I saw this morning.

As I looked at those small oak trees, I felt that the Lord was reminding me of His life giving creative power seen so clearly in nature, that also has its spiritual counterpart in us, in our new 'spirit life' within. We have been born again and the natural order of things will be for that new life to grow, and grow, unless we deliberately shut it down, by starving it of the sun – the love of God, nutrition – His words, and living water – the life of the Holy Spirit flowing through us.

Every time we feel that we have failed, or messed up, and every time that we feel that our growth has been stunted, let us thank Him for this wonderful principal of growth, natural and spiritual. I believe that as we turn away from our sense of failure, and even disappointment with ourselves, and turn instead to the Lord, to receive forgiveness (if we need to) and to thank Him for the grace and power of His new life within, we will grow some more.

When a young sapling is battered by the wind, or trying to survive during a time of drought, it will send its roots ever deeper into the earth in order to increase its stability. Longer deeper roots will also enable it to find the water and nutrients which it needs in order to thrive. Our thanksgiving in times of discouragement will be our way of sending our roots down further into God's love and grace. Our thanksgiving for this wonderful principal of growth will enable us to believe in and draw on this new life within.

Activation . . .

Thanksgiving will stop you relying on your own efforts to 'grow' yourself. It will enable you to humbly yield to His life within. It will enable you to agree with Jesus in a positive way when He said, "apart from me you can do nothing", (John 15:5). And so we circle back to recognising ourselves as those who need to 'abide in Him' at all times in order to grow and bear fruit. Thanksgiving for this principal of 'growth' may also help you to see yourself with the eyes of faith, as He sees you, not as a little sapling but as an 'oak of righteousness' that declares to our world something of who God Himself is.

DAY 290 | Thanksgiving and Our 'Seasons'

My morning walk, yet again, gave me the inspiration for today's reflection. This time I was struck by the beauty of the mellow autumn colours in the very welcome morning sunshine. As I was thanking the Lord for the lovely view ahead of me I just felt the Holy Spirit reminding me that there is beauty, not only in every season in nature, but in every season of life too. He was saying that I would see this beauty more clearly if I could be thankful for, and embrace, those seasons as they come.

When we are young a change of season can often be challenging, but exciting too; full of hope and expectancy. The changes come thick and fast – from adolescent to adult, school to uni., and from learning a skill or profession to entering the workplace. A change of season, even good changes, can also, of course, involve loss. Getting married for example and having a family, wonderful as those changes are, mean that we lose some freedom, time and probably energy to do the things we want. Moving into a new season, will involve changes and probably some element of 'loss' in terms of location and even in relationships.

It's so important therefore to recognise the biblical principal of seasons about which the preacher wrote, very graphically, in Ecclesiastes 3:1-8. He said, 'To everything there a season, and a time to every purpose under the heaven:' (AV) Life in all its different aspects is not simply a one way climb up a mountain, 'till we reach a peak and then stay there, walking tall and high. It is in fact more like a journey through undulating territory. In some seasons we get clear views ahead and in others we walk on in faith, not seeing far ahead, but trusting our heavenly Shepherd to lead and guide.

As life progresses we can all fear a change of season. We realise that life is not just going to move, humanly speaking, from 'good' to 'better' to 'best'. Changes often mean the death of one thing in order to make way for the arrival of another, and if we are honest we can want to hold onto that which we know, and dread the losses involved in change.

Spiritually we also travel through different seasons, and when we are transitioning from one season to another spiritually, as well as in life, it is important that we travel closely with our Friend and Helper 'the Holy Spirit'. As our spiritual seasons change, as with the physical changes, there will be things that we need to let go of in order to embrace the challenges and blessings of the next season.

Walking this morning and seeing the effect of the sun I realised that what can seem a bit dull and drab in nature is enhanced and even transformed by the sunshine. When the sun did come out the very ordinary scene at which I was looking, became something of great beauty. In the same way, thanksgiving for, and during, a time of change can really help me in my letting go, in my embracing of loss, and also in 'seeing' the beauty of the new possibilities, and the hand of God on my life in the new season. I believe thanksgiving for, and as, I travel through a change in season will, like the sunshine this morning, 'light it up' for me and reveal its beauty.

It reminded me of another passage in Ecclesiastes. Not only is there a time for everything, but God **'has made everything beautiful in its time.** He has also set eternity in the hearts of men; yet they cannot fathom what God has done from beginning to end. I know that there is nothing better than for men to be happy and to do good while they live. That everyone may eat and drink and find satisfaction in all his toil – this is the gift of God.' (Ecclesiastes 3:11-13).

Activation . . .

Today thank the Lord for the 'season' that you are in, both in life and spiritually, (they often, of course, mirror each other) and see how embracing this season with thanksgiving will shed new and wonderful light on your journey, just like the sunshine lit up the beauty of the autumn trees for me this morning as I walked .

DAY 291 | Thanksgiving and Becoming 'A Man or Woman for all Seasons'

Yesterday we read 'THERE IS a time for everything and a season for everything under the sun.' (Ecclesiastes 3:1-8) The 'preacher' then enunciates all the contrasting seasons through which our lives can travel. Have you noticed that our Christian lives go through seasons as do our natural lives? There are 'good', comfortable, positive seasons and some that feel more like times of loss and difficulty. It's important that we understand this and resist the common belief that, if we are doing things right, all aspects of life should just get better and better.

In the wilderness the Children of Israel had their freedom, but they had to cope with the loss of certain foods, the security of water and of course having a homeland. They did however live with the daily miracles of protection and provision. When they came into the Promised Land the Lord was very clear about a certain 'risk'. Indeed God had warned them against this in Deuteronomy 6:10-12. It was the risk that they would forget Him when life got easier in the Promised Land.

Now sometimes when things are tough and we don't feel very grateful we can think to ourselves, "when everything settles down and all these problems are behind me and everything is going well, when I get into a 'better' season of life, I'll be grateful all the time". Such is our nature as human beings, however, that times of plenty can also have a bad effect on our levels of gratitude, as we forget the hard times and all God's faithfulness and start to take everything that we have for granted, or even feel proud that we are doing well by our own strength. (Deuteronomy 8:7-18).

The risk is this: when we are in a difficult season we can grumble and not be grateful for, or even notice, the Lord's help, but then when everything is going well, we can be liable to forget the Lord's kindness and goodness to us. We can then find ourselves forgetting to honour Him, just as God's people did both in the wilderness and in the Promised Land "flowing with milk and honey". (Judges 3:7). Let's face it grumbling and complaining like the Children of Israel can happen in either season, and even in the boring in between times when life is simply jogging along and neither challenging us or overwhelming us.

Thanksgiving in times of need can be hard and we have reflected on this on previous days; however when we stand back and reflect, if we are honest, many of us can neglect thanksgiving when everything is going well. We forget to thank God for the many, many daily blessings that He showers upon us. We begin to take them for granted, and even saying 'thank you' for our meals may not have the force of gratitude that it had for our ancestors who knew the fragility of a good harvest.

In Proverbs 30:8,9 we read a wise prayer '. . . give me neither poverty nor riches, but give me only my daily bread. Otherwise I may have too much and disown you and say 'Who is the Lord?' Or I may become poor and steal, and so dishonour the name of my God.'

Activation . . .

Let 'thanksgiving' make you a man or woman for all seasons. Give intentional thanksgiving both in times of need, times of plenty, and the in between times. It will really help you in your walk with God. It will honour his name, and remind you of His goodness, great care and love for you daily. It will also greatly benefit your well-being.

Caleb, I believe, was a man who remembered His God, and all he had done, and he was ready and strong for a big fight at the grand age of 85! (Joshua 14:6-14). Read it and be encouraged! And specifically remember that, even in times of difficulty, we still have loads to thank God for. Jesus still died for us, we will always have the free gift of forgiveness, eternal life and much more.

DAY 292 | Thanksgiving and My Perspective

In Revelation 4:1 the Apostle John is invited to "Come up here." He is invited into the throne room of heaven in order to see and hear "... what must take place..." The implication being that he would not be able to grasp or comprehend what was going to happen, unless he saw it all unfolding from heaven's perspective.

There have been others like John who have been as it were 'taken to heaven', and who have seen into that realm, but for most of us, although we can 'in our spirits' discern heavenly things, heaven itself is an unseen realm that we will not encounter until we die. Never the less I believe that the Lord wants us to 'see' things more and more from a heavenly perspective. He wants us to see His hand on our lives and His dealings with us, to see His heart of love for ourselves and others, and to see how He works out His plans and purposes in the middle of the chaos that there seems to be all around us on the earth at this time.

We need 'vision' to see things like God does, even to see the spiritual realities that are all around us, like Elisha's servant. The situation for him was that the king of Aram, fed up with the fact that Elisha kept telling the King of Israel by word of knowledge, what he, the King of Aram, was planning privately in his bedroom, ordered the capture of Elisha. He had sent horses and chariots to surround the city of Dothan where Elisha and his servant were. The servant on getting up in the morning saw that the city was surrounded, and quite understandably panicked saying "Oh, my lord what shall we do?"

Elisha said "Don't be afraid. Those who are with us are more than those who are with them." Then he prayed a simple prayer, "O Lord, open his eyes so he may see." And of course he does see. He sees the hills full of horses and chariots of fire. (2 Kings 6:8-18). Now not many of us have had our spiritual eyes opened in this way, although we have heard recently of friends – missionaries in what is now a very dangerous country for Christians – who have actually seen their angelic protectors. For most of us, however, having our perspective altered from an earthly one to a heavenly one is less dramatic but equally important.

We have stated many times, throughout this year, that thanksgiving is the key that unlocks the gate into that heavenly realm; the key that opens the way into God's presence, (Psalm 100:4), and it can also open up our spirit to 'hear' and commune with the Holy Spirit; to begin to 'see' what God is up to in our lives. This is the sentiment expressed in a wonderful song on the Bethel album 'Be lifted High'[1].

It begins, 'God I look to you, I won't be overwhelmed. Give me vision to see things like you do. God I look to you, you're where my help comes from, give me wisdom, you know just what to do.' The song ends with the words, 'Hallelujah our God reigns'. At one point in the middle, the singer Jenn Johnson encourages, 'Thanks and Praise, Thanks and Praise', and that surely is the key to transitioning from, 'God I look to you and I won't be overwhelmed' to being able to make that declaration 'My God reigns'. I know that has been the case for me on many occasions.

John, the same one who was caught up into heaven to 'see what must take place', wrote to some early Christians about those who were carrying the spirit of antichrist. He encourages them with these words, 'You dear children, are from God and have overcome them, because the one who is in you is greater than the one who is in the world.' (1 John 4:4). It's a verse we have probably all used at some point to encourage ourselves or others. Thanking God, that this really is the truth, will help us to believe it.

Activation . . .

Whether you feel that you are in a battle that is spiritual like those Christians that John was addressing, or physical as it was for Elisha, or if you are feeling confused and uncertain about things in your own life and family, or if you would simply like to 'see' and 'hear' the heavenly perspective on different situations, 'give thanks' for it will surely lift your gaze to heaven. Thanksgiving will direct your heart to the love and power of God in your life, and the lives of others (See Psalm 62:11,12). Thanksgiving will allow the Holy Spirit to fill your mind and heart with truth and with God's perspective on whatever it is that is concerning you at this time.

DAY 293 | Thanksgiving and a Higher Perspective

Yesterday we were sharing about the need to get a higher perspective on life. On the need to see things from God's perspective, especially those things in our personal circumstances, and world events, that can trouble us. Today as I was out walking I felt that the Lord was saying that we need this higher perspective – His perspective – on the people around us too. A higher perspective, both of those in the family of God, and others (our friends, neighbours, family and work colleagues,) who are not yet in the Kingdom.

I think that the Lord wants this because it is just so often our default setting to see what is wrong with someone, to see their faults, weaknesses and mistakes and how they need to change. It's often much easier to see those things, than the 'gold' that is often buried a little deeper inside. If we are to fulfill Jesus' command to 'Love each another as I have loved you' (John 15:12), we are most certainly going to need to 'see' each other in the way that Jesus sees us. Likewise in order to follow Paul's teaching on our relationships, (see Day 330), we are going to need the indwelling Holy Spirit to open our eyes to the treasure that is in each one.

I love that Jesus was so wise. His teaching covers so many of our human weaknesses. Consider Matthew 7:1-5 about not judging others. This passage contains the famous exhortation to deal with the plank in our own eye before taking the speck out of our brother's eye. It does not say we shouldn't help our brother with his speck but it does in effect say, 'sort yourself out first!' Well, it's true isn't it? Very often what we notice about each other, what we observe as another's faults and failings, has an echo in our own lives that we can't fully see.

Sometimes it's not that we have exactly the same issue, but that when I am irritated or upset by someone else, it highlights something in me that the Lord is seeking to refine. I first discovered this principle as a youngish Christian, when the Lord encouraged me to thank Him for someone I was finding difficult. He said in effect that I could be thankful for that person because, through them, He was going to do a work of grace in my life that wouldn't happen if they weren't there. It's the principal of the 'grit in the oyster' that produces the beautiful pearl.

Thanksgiving in such a situation frees up the Holy Spirit to pinpoint the area in me that He wants to refine. Thanksgiving also, as we said yesterday, lifts our gaze to gain heavens perspective thereby allowing the Holy Spirit to fill us again with His wisdom, insight and redemptive love, as we walk alongside our brothers and our sisters. And so in these challenging situations, and indeed in all our relationships, having the Lord's perspective is vital if we are to truly love one another, and look for the best in each other.

The wonderful lyrics in Geoff Bullock's song 'Lord I come to you'[1], remind me that when I wait on the Lord, when I let His love surround me, I can 'soar with Him' like the eagle, (Isaiah 40:31), and see things as He does. He will 'unveil my eyes,' giving me a better perspective on my own 'stuff' so that, first and foremost, He can help me to change and become more like Him in my attitudes and behavior.

The truth is that as I let the Lord's unconditional love and grace change me, I am more likely to be filled with God's own love and grace towards others. This is transformational love. It is powerful, and it is, I think, the love that Paul wrote of when he spoke of us growing up into Christ, 'from whom the whole body, being fitted and held together by what every joint supplies, according to the proper working of each individual part, causes the growth of the body for **the building up of itself in love.**' (Ephesians 4:16, NASB). And it all starts, I believe, with turning in our hearts to thank the Lord for each other daily.

Activation . . .

Learn to thank God for the people in your life, 'warts and all', and see how it opens your eyes to see the gems and the good things that they bring into your life. It will take your gaze off of any weaknesses and failings, and allow you to celebrate, not just who God has made them to be, but also who God intends them to become.

DAY 294 | Thanksgiving and Discipline

So hands up who likes being 'told off'. That is so often what we associate with discipline; someone telling us what we have done wrong. Being 'disciplined' reminds us of being 'bad', and being punished. So the words 'discipline' and 'love' don't always sit comfortably together in our world where even saying 'no' to a child can be seen as negative and controlling. Well that frame of reference does not apply to our heavenly Father who, we are told, 'disciplines those whom He loves.'

The word discipline speaks of training and learning, and if we reckon on ourselves being Jesus' 'disciples', we have clearly signed up for the teaching and training that that will involve. Jesus twelve disciples often found themselves being corrected by Jesus, but with what love and wisdom? He never put them down, but always sought to show them 'the better way'. So we are told that while it may not feel great, 'God disciplines us for our good, that we may share in His holiness.' (Hebrews 12:5-12). God disciplines or 'trains' us so that we may become a 'partaker of His divine nature', and live more fully from our 'new life' in Christ. It's all to make us more like Jesus. How wonderful! Truly something for which we can be very grateful.

When the disciples were arguing about who would be the greatest, Jesus shows them a little child and teaches them that 'the greatest among you should be like the youngest and the one who rules like the one who serves.' (Luke 22:24-27). He taught, then demonstrated servant leadership to them by taking the towel and washing their feet when no one else seemed to want to. (John 13:4-17). He rebuked them when they wanted to call down fire on a village that did not welcome Him. (Luke 9:51-56). But He never gave up on them, or shamed them unkindly.

If we can see that all of the Lord's disciplining of us comes from His heart of love, and from His intense desire to grow us into mature sons and daughters and make us like Himself, then we can welcome His discipline and allow it to reaffirm our place in His Father's heart. As the writer to the Hebrews points out, 'If you are not disciplined then you are illegitimate children and not true sons.' (Hebrews 12:7,8). The writer also encourages those feeling wearied by the Lord's discipline in their lives to strengthen themselves and not cave in, for example, to self pity. (My interpretation of verses 12 and 13.)

If we need biblical evidence of God's love for us when we are being corrected, then we need look no further than how Jesus spoke to the Laodicean church. (Revelation 3:14-21). This church, it would appear, was not 'on fire'. On the contrary they were so half hearted that Jesus uses a very graphic picture of 'spitting them out of His mouth'. Quite a stinging rebuke! One at which many of us, in our day, might well take offence. He then, in what would be an uncomfortable conversation for any of us, goes on to point out that they are quite deluded about how well they are doing.

But if we listen to the conversation a little longer, we hear not just the stinging rebuke but the love and longing in His heart to bring them close and to give them all that they need to become the people He is looking for them to be. There is no Sergeant Major tone here. 'Get your act together'. 'Buck up'. 'Work a bit harder'. Instead we hear an incredible offer, "Come and get what you need, faith, spiritual riches, garments of splendour, eye salve – fresh revelation", and I also hear an echo of Isaiah 55:1,2 'Come buy ... without money or cost.' What an amazing offer.

He then says those wonderful words, **'Those whom I love I rebuke and discipline'**. "I am being this strong with you because I love you." The atmosphere in this church might make Him 'sick', but He loves them so, so much that He wants change, and the change He most wants is for them to welcome Him right back into the centre of their hearts and lives. 'Here I am!' He says, 'I stand at the door and knock. If anyone hears my voice and opens the door, I will come in and eat with him, and he with me.' Now that is what I call a wonderful offer of restored closeness. One none of us could refuse.

Activation ...

Let your gratitude help you to receive discipline with joy and expectancy from the hand of your loving Father who just wants your best – ALWAYS!!! Thanksgiving will keep your heart soft and open, to His rebuke, and responsive and quick to learn. It will also position you to enjoy the pleasure of an 'intimate meal' with Him. (Revelation 3:20). Yes! Being thankful for the discipline of the Lord is a wise and fruitful way to go.

DAY 295 | Thanksgiving and Moving Forward

We reminded ourselves yesterday that the Lord always, ALWAYS, disciplines us out of love, and with redemption in His heart. He always disciplines us with the intention of bringing us, day by day, closer to Himself and to our destiny of becoming more like Jesus. Sometimes we have a difficulty receiving that love, and accepting ourselves as learners, (disciples). We can be very perfectionist with ourselves and find it hard to get past a mistake we have made, or a sin we have committed.

In the middle of his second letter to the Corinthian church, Paul gives us a personal, vulnerable, and interesting insight into an aspect of his journey with the Lord. He tells us that when he came to Troas with the gospel of Christ, the Lord 'opened a door' for him; a great opportunity to share the gospel. Nonetheless he had no rest in his spirit because he could not find his brother Titus. So, notwithstanding the great opportunity, he took his leave of the people in Troas and went on into Greece. (See 2 Corinthians 2:12,13). On the face of it seems as though Paul had missed a great opportunity, for surely, taking that chance to preach was more important than finding Titus!

So what is Paul's response? 'But thanks be to God, who always leads us in triumph in Christ and manifests through us the sweet aroma of the knowledge of Him in every place.' (verse 14, NASB). Now if I am honest, I find it hard to imagine myself doing that. I think, on past experience, that there is a real risk that I would have gone into regret, even beaten myself up for missing the opportunity.

So how did Paul deal with this situation? Not by rationalisation, self-justification, multiple excuses, or self recrimination, but with thanksgiving. And not just thanksgiving by rote, or thanksgiving because he ought to do it, or thanksgiving because he had read all of the books on 'Thanksgiving' and knew what a good Christian should do! No he moved into thanksgiving because he saw that God was bigger than he Paul, in his humanity and frailty. He knew that God would continue to lead him in triumph every day.

He was going to continue on his journey and express all that God had given him to the people that he met. In fact, if we read on, we find that Paul says quite a lot about his weakness and vulnerability, but also about God's greatness, God's strength made perfect in his weakness, and the treasure of the life of Christ that was in the clay pot of his humanity. He knew the God who makes 'His light shine in our hearts to give the light of the knowledge of the glory of God in the face of Jesus Christ'. (2 Corinthians 4:1-7).

I'm sure this thrilled the Lord's heart as He saw Paul grasping the greatness of his grace and power, and his forgiveness when needed. Thanksgiving for this powerful grace prevented Paul going into decline, or doing any penance. It resulted in Paul continuing in faith that the Lord was indeed 'leading him in triumph' to bless other people. It resulted in him fully sharing the gospel when he arrived in the next place. In fact Paul was practicing what he preached, '... one thing I do. Forgetting what lies behind and straining toward what lies ahead, I press on towards the goal to win the prize for which God has called me heavenward in Christ Jesus.' (Philippians 3:13,14).

We can see here that thanksgiving is a very powerful way of putting into practice 'the leaving the past behind' that Paul advocates. Let's be honest it's not always easy to forget what lies behind, especially if I feel that I failed or didn't do too well; but thanksgiving is a very practical help in doing this. It's important to realise that this is not positive thinking or whitewash, because our thanksgiving is for real truths, including that God is a pardoning and forgiving God, (Micah 7:18,19) and that He, the Lord, will work all things for the good of those who love him. It was His idea to put His treasure in these common clay pots – us! He is full of grace and able to continue to flow through us, because Christ in us is our hope of glory. (See Colossians 1:27).

Activation ...

When we 'miss it', or **think** we have 'missed it', we can easily become disappointed with ourselves, but not if we get a vision of the greatness and the grace of God, and the awesome truth that He has put the treasure of His life in the 'clay pot' that is me. (2 Corinthians 4:7). Take those opportunities today to follow Paul's example and move into thanksgiving, even when you feel you have tripped up.

DAY 296 | Thanksgiving for Jesus' Authority

As a family we have been much amused over the years by reading *The Sacred Diary of Adrian Plass*.[1] I am recalling the time when, challenged by the thought that 'faith can move a mountain', Adrian decides to practice privately on something small and discreet. He chooses a paper clip and 'commands' it to move across the table. Unfortunately, not only does the paper clip not move, but his wife and son are convulsed with laughter outside the door, as they overhear his efforts to 'move' this tiny object 'by faith'. Well, we all know that moving any inanimate object, large or small, will take real faith, but let's not knock the thought here that someone was willing to step out and practice, because growing in faith is always going to involve taking a risk.

Our world is so full of need however, that we really don't need to practice on a paper clip. Let us instead be moved with compassion and bring the love of God into our family, our workplace and our neighbourhood. Let us not be fearful but thankful for every opportunity to 'practice', and for every opportunity to learn and to grow in faith. Most people these days will be glad if you offer to pray for them if they have a need; glad that someone cares, and if they aren't pleased, you will have at least sown a seed in their heart that, 'Just maybe there is a God who loves them and who could help them.' A seed that may germinate at a later date.

There is no doubt in the minds of most of God's people that Jesus has risen from the dead and ascended to the highest possible place in all of heaven and earth. We know this because Paul tells us that having humbled Himself to the point of allowing Himself to die a criminal's death on the cross, 'God exalted him to the highest place and gave him the name that is above every name, that at the name of Jesus every knee should bow, in heaven and on earth and under the earth, and every tongue confess that Jesus Christ is Lord, to the glory of God the Father.' (Philippians 2:8-11).

This is a really important truth to hold onto in an age when the name of Jesus is very frequently used as a swear word, and when the internet world is full of 'influencers' who use their name and ideas to gather huge numbers of 'followers'. The problem for them is that their fame is only temporal, and will only last for a season. Our Jesus, our King of Kings, 'will be called, 'Wonderful Counselor, Mighty God, Everlasting Father, Prince of Peace,' forever and ever, and furthermore, 'Of the increase of His government and peace there will be no end.' (Isaiah 9:6,7). Now that is good news!

The apostle John, in his vision of heaven, saw the throne and heard these same truths sung by all the creatures in heaven and earth. "To him who sits on the throne and to the Lamb be praise and honor and glory and power, for ever and ever!" (Revelation 5:13). As far as our triune God is concerned, Father, Son and Holy Spirit, the victory has been won. Verifying that Jesus was definitely not just an angel, the writer to the Hebrews asks the question, 'To which of the angels did God ever say, "Sit at my right hand until I make your enemies a footstool for your feet"?' (Hebrews 1:13), thus indicating that the victory, now being celebrated in heaven, will one day become apparent on the earth.

Jesus was raised from the dead by God's Mighty Power, 'which he exerted in Christ when he raised him from the dead and seated him at his right hand in the heavenly realms, far above all rule and authority, power and dominion, and every title that can be given, not only in the present age but also in the one to come. And God placed all things under His feet and appointed Him to be head over everything for the church, which is His body, the fullness of Him who fills everything in every way.' (Ephesians 1:20-23).

Mysteriously, and mystically, we who have accepted God's love and forgiveness through Christ; we who have made Him the Lord of our lives, have also been raised up with Christ and seated with Him in the heavenly realms in Christ Jesus. (Ephesians 2:6). We are now part of His plan to make "the kingdom of the world ... the Kingdom of our Lord and of His Christ, and he will reign for ever and ever." (Revelation 11:15).

Activation ...

Today thank the Lord for every opportunity to 'practice' stepping out in faith. And as you step out remind yourself of the immense power and authority that Jesus has. Remember these scriptures that we have shared today and thank Him, before you start to pray, that He has won!!

DAY 297 | Thanksgiving and Our Authority

Jesus was clear about His authority, and one of the last things He said to His disciples was, "All authority in heaven and on earth has been given to me. Therefore go and make disciples of all nations, baptizing them in the name of the Father and of the Son and of the Holy Spirit, and teaching them to obey everything I have commanded you. And surely I am with you always, to the very end of the age." (Matthew 28:18-20). By saying **therefore** at that point, He was clearly conveying to them that the authority that He had was going to be theirs. If it wasn't they would just be on a hiding to nothing, trying to start a movement but not actually transforming lives.

Jesus also conveyed to them at this time that although His physical body was not going to be seen on earth anymore, His presence was going to be with them. Now these disciples had seen Jesus power at work, and had already tasted the power that He had given them when they used His name with authority. In those heady days they had returned to Him saying "Lord even the demons submit to us in your name." (Luke 10:17). But that was when Jesus was there in the flesh, as their teacher and mentor. Now He tells them that it is going to be better for them that He is going to go away, because He is going to send the Holy Spirit. (John 16:7). How amazing is that?

He said of the Spirit, "you know him, for he lives with you, and **will be in you**,' (John 14:17 and see John 20:22). Before He ascended He again reminded them of His promise saying, "Do not leave Jerusalem, but wait for the gift my Father promised, which you have heard me speak about. For John baptized you with water but in a few days you will be baptized (immersed) with the Holy Spirit." (Acts 1:4,5). And the rest is history. Pentecost came, and the Holy Spirit came too. He came upon the disciples with power, and the young church exploded into life as the apostles preached and did 'many wonders and miraculous signs.' (Acts 2:43).

In the Acts of the Apostles we read how the early church 'turned the world upside down', (Acts 17:6, AV), as they moved with authority and power, preaching, teaching, healing and doing miracles in Jesus' name. The

Kingdom of God spread far and wide wherever they went. So what about us 2000 years later? We read that when Jesus was on earth, He had authority over the natural world, (John 2:1-11), over the demonic, (Luke 4:33-36), over death, (Luke 7:14,15), over religious systems, (Luke 6:6-10), and over lives where people welcomed His teaching in their hearts and minds. (Luke 19:2-10). This is the authority that He has delegated to us, His people.

When Jesus was with the disciples one time and they were having difficulty casting a demon out of a little boy, He said to them that their failure in this instance was "because you have so little faith. I tell you the truth, if you have faith as small as a mustard seed, you can say to this mountain, "Move from here to there" and it will move. Nothing will be impossible for you." (Matthew 17:20-23). I personally feel that I need to stand there with those disciples and receive that challenge from the Lord, because I believe that the Lord is calling us in these days to a level of faith and authority that most of us have never experienced.

Let us thank Him that He said that **'therefore'** to His disciples before telling them what they were to do. That He still says that **'therefore'** to us "All authority in heaven and on earth has been given to me. **Therefore** go and make disciples of all nations..." If we fully grasp these truths, we can go in His name with His delegated authority; otherwise we would just be working hard in our own strength, relying on the power of persuasion.

Activation ...

Yesterday we started to practice moving in a greater level of faith by thanking Jesus, that He is on the throne, and that we are 'seated with Him'. Today I think it is about believing that, because of the outpoured and indwelling Holy Spirit, that same authority has been delegated to us. Thank the Lord today for all the areas over which He exercised His authority, teaching the disciples to do the same. Thank God for the wonderful truth that we are not just His representatives on the earth, but that we also carry His authority as we speak 'in Jesus name'. We have the indwelling Holy Spirit with us, the 'dunamis' of God to release into our world. So let us grow in faith and ask big prayers, worthy of our big God, in line with the authority that He has delegated to us, (Matthew 6:9,10), and the power He has placed within us.

DAY 298 | Thanksgiving and Moving in 'Faith'

We have been sharing about the commission that Jesus gave to us, His followers, to spread His Kingdom throughout the earth. We have seen that we can build our faith with thanksgiving that Jesus has "All authority in heaven and on earth", and that He followed that with "Therefore . . ." as He now includes us, His disciples, in this task of 'making disciples of all nations'. We can thank Him that He is now seated in the highest place and has the name that is above all names, and that He promises to be with us, empowering us with His outpoured and indwelling Spirit. One further ingredient is needed however if we are to fulfill this commission and 'move in faith'. After Jesus said "therefore", He also said "go". The fact is that we are never going to see His kingdom spread and His power manifest, if we don't 'go'!

We have already talked about the need to practice and to step out boldly in order to grow in faith, because wherever we look, whatever walk of life they are in, people become good at what they do if they practice. I think that's why Jesus sent out the twelve, (Luke 9:1-6) and then the seventy two, (Luke 10:1-11). We read that they came back rejoicing, but who knows that they didn't make their mistakes, or flunk a few opportunities. We only have one recorded failure as such, (Mark 9:17,18) but there were other times when they would have sent people, or children away when it was Jesus plan to bless. (Luke 9:12, Matthew 19:13,14). We can clearly be encouraged by the fact that Jesus never gave up on them. He just corrected them and taught them a better way.

So what does 'go' look like for us? Most of us have jobs, family and other responsibilities and we are not called to travel around as was Paul, or become 'full-time' in ministry. We are however in daily contact with people who have not as yet come into the Kingdom. In Luke 10:8,9, we hear Jesus teaching the disciples how to approach the task He set before them. He said, "When you enter a town and are welcomed, eat what is set before you. Heal the sick who are there and tell them 'the Kingdom of God is near you.'" I believe He is saying, in effect, go where you are welcomed into someone's life, however briefly. Respond with warmth and friendship. See what their needs are and release the appropriate blessing – then you can tell them about the God who can meet that need.

Being welcomed into someone's life might not necessarily be about going into their home for a meal. It could be a momentary conversation, or a meeting at the supermarket. It may only last a few moments, but to the extent that someone has welcomed you into their world, you may also be able to find out what their concern is. Healing is not necessarily the top priority for people these days, (they trust the NHS), but rather it may be loneliness, worry about their children or their finances; the job that they can't get, or the job they have, but hate. Whatever it is, we can tell them that there is a God who can help them, and we can pray and release blessing as God's representatives here on earth.

Sometimes I believe we are hesitant to engage with people in this way because we are afraid that 'nothing will happen' if we pray. We don't want to disappoint, (or to look foolish ourselves.) The truth is that if we pray 'in His name' something is definitely going to happen. We don't have to predict what God will do if we haven't got that measure of faith, i.e. "If I pray God will definitely heal you", but we can offer to ask God to help them. I heard a while ago of someone who was sick, who was prayed for. He was not healed (at that time!) but said that he had never felt so loved. The world is so full of need we really don't need to practice on a paper clip. Let us instead be moved with compassion and bring the love of God into our family, our workplace and our neighbourhood. Let us be alert to those moments of opportunity when we are welcomed into someone's life, however briefly, and be ready to share His love.

Activation . . .

Be thankful for every opportunity to 'practice', for every opportunity to learn and to grow in faith. Thanking the Lord for that opportunity will prevent you from 'shrinking back' in unbelief. Then ask big prayers, worthy of your big God, and if nothing else comes to mind you can still pray as He taught us, 'Lord in this situation, may Your Kingdom come, Your will be done, here and now on earth in line with your will in heaven'. (Matthew 6:9,10).

DAY 299 | Thanksgiving for My New heart

We watched a strange film the other night. It was about a young woman who had a heart transplant. Ever since she'd had the transplant she didn't feel 'herself'. 'Herself' being an angry, promiscuous, very selfish person with a broken career, toxic family relationships, no real place to call home, a job she hates and ruined friendships.

Out of the blue, she meets a stranger who makes her feel 'safe' and who helps her to live a different kind of life. He suggests she tries to be kind, which leads to the healing of old family wounds. She turns her talents to helping the homeless and, as time goes by, she finally realises that this illusive stranger is the 'man' whose heart she received as a transplant. It's his heart that now keeps her alive. Yes I know! It's quite a freaky thought, and not remotely possible in the real world, but as I pondered it, it seemed to be a very good picture that could help us to understand our 'new life in Christ'.

After the transplant the woman says, rather bitterly, "They took my old heart and threw it away. And now I don't feel myself." Then the man who died and effectively gave her his heart, appears and helps her to live with this new heart. So Jesus died in our place, and we died to our old self when we gave our lives to Him. Our 'old heart' was 'taken away', and He gave us a new one, **His** life! 'I have been crucified with Christ and I no longer live, but Christ lives in me. The life I live in the body, I live by faith in the Son of God who loved me and gave himself for me.' (Galatians 2:20).

Jesus gave His life that we might become a new creation! But that is not all. In order to help us to understand, and live out of our new life, He sent the Holy Spirit to come along side as our helper. He guides us into being kind and loving, patient and faithful. He indwells us in order that we should live as Jesus would, (1 John 2:6), not because we are trying hard to follow His rules, but because we have a new heart, **His** heart, firmly planted deep within us.

This truth is why we can be confident and have absolute faith that He is not trying to improve the 'old', but that He has given us a completely new heart which now enables us to live a completely new life. This is why we can 'put off the old and put on the new.' It's now a choice. We have a new nature and we no longer have to live according to our old ways and habits.

Sometimes we can choose to revert to our old and familiar ways, but we now carry His heart in this world, and need to live as He would. So here are some scriptures to confirm us in these truths starting with an Old Testament promise of the New Covenant to come:- 'I will give you a new heart and put a new spirit within you; I will remove from you your heart of stone and give you a heart of flesh. And I will put my Spirit in you and move you to follow my decrees and be careful to keep my laws.' (Ezekiel 36:26,27).

'We were therefore buried with Him through baptism into death in order that, just as Christ was raised from the dead through the glory of the Father, we too might live a new life. If we have been united with Him like this in His death, we will certainly also be united with Him in His resurrection. For we know that our old self was crucified with Him so that the body of sin might be done away with, that we should no longer be slaves to sin – because anyone who has died has been freed from sin . . . In the same way, count yourselves dead to sin but alive to God in Jesus Christ. Therefore do not let sin reign in your mortal body, . . . but rather offer yourselves to God, as those who have been bought from death to life; . . . as instruments of righteousness.' (Romans 6:4-13). 'Therefore, if anyone is in Christ, he is a new creation; the old has gone, the new has come!' (2 Corinthians 5:17).

'You were taught, with regard to your former way of life, to put off your old self, which is being corrupted by its sinful desires; to be made new in the attitude of your minds; and to put on the new self, created to be like God in true righteousness and holiness.' (Ephesians 4:22). 'Do not lie to each other, since you have taken off your old self with its practices and have put on the new self, which is being renewed in the image of its creator.' (Colossians 3:9)

Activation . . .

Today thank God for your completely 'new life' in Christ, it will help you to 'live by faith' out of that new life. Thanking God for this 'heart transplant' will keep you from trying to be a better person in your own strength, and it will help you to draw, with the Holy Spirit's help, on His new life that is already within you.

DAY 300 | Thanksgiving and My New Heart

Yesterday we were considering the miracle of 'new birth' and the fact that the Lord has taken away our old stony heart and given us His heart. He has also given us His Spirit in order to help us to live from that new heart, without returning to the old. The apostle Paul, on several occasions, felt the need to spell out to the young Christians of his day exactly what that would look like, and in Galatians we have that beautiful list of all the fruit of the Spirit, contrasted with the 'works' of the flesh. (Galatians 5:19-23).

In Colossians he encourages the Christians to 'put to death' their earthly nature, (which he then lists), and to 'put on', to clothe themselves, with some very lovely qualities which are in essence the same qualities as the fruit of the Spirit mentioned above. (Colossians 3:7-15). To the Ephesians he wrote, 'You were taught, with regard to your former way of life, to put off your old self, which is being corrupted by its sinful desires; to be made new in the attitude of your minds; and to put on the new self, created to be like God in true righteousness and holiness.' (Ephesians 4:22,23).

Now Paul clearly noticed a struggle going on in the members of the early church. A struggle with which he, and probably all of us can, identify, (Romans 7:21-23). I have a new heart, I am a new creation, and yet I sometimes behave like I'm not, and that I haven't been given a new heart. For Paul winning that battle often came down to two things; firstly recognising that there is a choice, i.e. my will is involved here, and secondly that what I allow into my mind is a key to the kind of choice that I make.

I believe that one of the difficulties in living from our 'new heart', or the 'new me in Christ' is that most of the information that we collect day by day comes through our five senses, or through our memory. All day long we are hearing things, seeing things, reading things, absorbing things, or remembering things, that, if we are not careful, can simply 'trigger' our 'old man' reactions. We may find ourselves getting angry, frightened, irritated, impatience, lustful, etc. etc. So a keen sense of injustice can turn into 'it's not fair'. Noticing someone else's good fortune can turn into jealousy.

Hearing the news can feed our anxiety. Picking up an insult, however veiled or unintentional, can stir anger, or self rejection, and so on and so on. In other words we need to be careful that what comes to us through our mind, and into our hearts, doesn't get to stir up the 'old me', but gets to come through and be processed by the 'new me'. So how do we do that?

It seems to me that it is about becoming strong in our spirit. Because we are now spiritual beings, we get to gather information not just through our five senses but through our spirit too. It is through our spirit that we hear the Holy Spirit guiding us, checking us, reminding us of the fruit that He wants to produce in our lives. We hear His reminders from the Word of God that we have hidden our hearts, (Psalm 119:11). In each and every situation we want to hear from the Holy Spirit loud and clear, both in our spirit and our mind, so that we can then choose to live from the 'new' us, not the 'old'.

I think that there are several ways to become 'strong' in our spirit. When encouraging the right use of the gift of tongues Paul said, 'He who speaks in a tongue edifies himself', that is to say they build themselves up, (I Corinthians 14:4). He said, 'I thank God that I speak in tongues more than all of you.' (1 Corinthians 14:18), so no wonder that he was tuned into the leading of the Holy Spirit, strong in His faith and determined to follow the Lord. We too can use the gift of tongues to 'build ourselves up'.

Another very important way in which to feed our spirit is to fill our minds with the truths from the Word of God. The Holy Spirit can then use those words to renew our minds. We can also build ourselves up by joining with others to come into the Lord's presence through worship. This will help to make sure that we are continually being filled with the Holy Spirit as we, 'Sing and make music in our heart to the Lord.' And 'Speak to one another with psalms, hymns and spiritual songs.' (Ephesians 5:19). Finally we can build up our spirit by, 'always giving thanks to God the Father for everything, in the name of our Lord Jesus Christ.' (Ephesians 5:20). And this is very good news because it means that we can choose to build ourselves up in our spirit anywhere, at any time, with or without anyone else around.

Activation . . .

Make a point, today, of continually building yourself up in your spirit and see for yourself how much easier living from the 'New You' becomes.

DAY 301 | More about My New Heart

We said yesterday that we need to keep our spirits strong in order to guard our minds and hearts from being overly influenced by everything that comes at us from the world through our five senses. The need to guard our hearts becomes even more urgent when times are tough, because in tough times we can feel self pity, critical of others, disappointed with ourselves, challenged in our faith and many other negative things, none of which do us any good. And even worse, these feelings and thoughts can smother the life in our 'new heart' making us revert back to some of our old ways. In Proverbs 4:23 we read 'Above all else guard your heart, for it is the wellspring of life.' Then, in 1Thessalonians 5:18, we have this incredible challenge from Paul. He says '... give thanks in all circumstances for this is God's will for you in Christ Jesus.' And I believe that for those of us with a new heart these two biblical injunctions are inextricably linked, so let's have a look at how exactly that works.

In hard circumstances we can hear ourselves thinking, "Surely 'giving thanks' can't really be what God is expecting of me? I need to fight these circumstances not express gratitude." But yes it is exactly what He is asking of us! And the Amplified Bible puts this challenge to us even more clearly. We read, 'Thank [God] in everything [no matter what the circumstances may be, be thankful and give thanks]. For this is the will of God for you [who are] in Christ Jesus [the Revealer and Mediator of that will].' So what is the link between guarding our hearts and giving thanks in all our difficult circumstances, and why does God tell us that this is His will for us?

First of all we need to realise that God is not being glib, nor is He telling us not to fight when he encourages us to give thanks in all circumstances. This is because **'giving thanks' is one of the most profound weapons that we have in our armoury**. It is a weapon that will neutralise the power of the enemy, (who probably instigated the bad circumstances in the first place). Giving thanks is the way to guard our heart and fight for our spiritual life. Now let's be clear, we are not thanking God **for** tragedy or **for** evil things happening, we are giving our thanks **'in the midst'** (TPT) of these circumstances because, as we do that, the sanctifying power and grace of God can come into those circumstances, and God will work in them and through them for His glory and our good. (Romans 8:28). So let's have a look at what thanksgiving in difficult circumstances does.

Firstly thanksgiving, as we have said on numerous days, and in different ways, is a God given way of staying 'present' with God. It stops us from shutting off from Him. In fact it does quite the opposite, it makes a way for Him to come into that situation that is causing us trouble or pain. Secondly 'thanksgiving' keeps us connected to our history with God, and so builds our faith for the 'now' as we express our trust in His unfailing love. As John Newton wrote in another of his hymns, so many years ago now, 'His love in times past, forbids me to think, He'll leave me at last in trouble to sink.'

Thirdly 'giving thanks' in those tough circumstances sanctifies and decontaminates our hearts from the lies that the enemy would implant at those times. It cleanses us from any suspicious thoughts about God's faithfulness. (See Jeremiah 15:19, AMP, which we explored on Day 283). Thanksgiving enables us to yield to God the difficult things in our lives, thereby placing them under His amazing grace. Fourthly, though probably not finally (because you may find many other ways in which thanksgiving helps you in these times), giving thanks brings deliverance as it immerses evil in the goodness of God. This is how we 'guard our hearts' in those stress filled times, in the middle of the storms of life. (See Psalm 50:23).

Now please note that I have deliberately written, many times, 'giving thanks' or 'thanksgiving' where I could have just simply written 'thankfulness'. This is because I believe we really need to be proactive in this process if we are to fully guard our hearts. We need to be radical with ourselves in the fight, because when we find ourselves in a place where we feel like we can't actively 'give thanks', consoling ourselves with the thought, 'Well I am grateful really', we leave ourselves open to the enemy, who will gladly come and start building a stronghold of lies in our heart.

Activation ...

Determine today to 'guard your heart' by proactively giving thanks in all the difficult parts of your life, and discover the miracle of God's transforming power as it works in your life in the hardest of times. Give Him thanks for His love, His faithfulness, for past deliverances and, perhaps most of all, that He is with you in the storm however it feels and whatever its cause.

DAY 302 | Thanksgiving and the Ten Commandments (Part 1)

We noted a couple of days ago that God's Word hidden in our hearts is a good way to guard our minds and our very selves from being tempted and deceived by the devil into reacting from the 'old me' and not the new creation that I now am. (Psalm 119:11). Another famous part of scripture that will help us is the Ten Commandments.

Often people these days say that the Ten Commandments are negative; full of things that we must **not** do. Keeping them will limit the fun, pleasure and freedom in life. Some even say that they paint a negative picture of God. This view is of course particularly prevalent among non Christians and people who would emphasise the need for so called 'freedom' and 'being yourself'. The feeling is that no one should be telling anyone else how to live their life. These thoughts can, however, permeate our Christian minds too. 'That's the Old Testament' we say and quickly move on to Jesus in the New!

But is this right? Are the Ten Commandments all negative? And should we down play them; embarrassed to own them as the best code of life that mankind has? Perhaps we need to look at them afresh with the understanding that **every 'no' actually carries a strong 'yes' with it**.

So let's look again at the Ten Commandments with a more positive lens!

1. 'Have no other Gods'. A 'no' here means a 'yes' to: – love the Lord with all your heart, soul and mind and strength, (Mark 12.30). Like Jesus said, you can't serve two masters, (Matthew 6:24), even though as humans we try to! Your 'no' to other gods is 'yes' to loving the Lord and discovering His love for you. Kind of positive?

2. Do not make idols or images. I think this builds on number 1. If I start loving money too much in my heart, I can get on the slippery slope of "what shall I use my money for next"? – Sparkly new car, house, kitchen etc. And, as it did for the rich young ruler, it can start to hamper, or even block my ability to walk freely with Jesus. This 'no' says 'yes' to nothing coming between me and Jesus. It says 'Yes' to my relationship with Jesus coming first. (Philippians 3:12-14).

3. Do not take God's name in vain. Here we need to understand that His name conveys the essence of who He is. This 'no' is a 'yes' to being blessed by using His name solely to drink in His character, and then to use the authority of His name to bless others very positively.

4. Do not work on the Sabbath day. This 'no' is a 'yes' to spiritually entering your rest as a fully 'redeemed by grace, through faith person', no works or self effort here. It's also practically about saying 'yes' to God's wonderful idea of having a day of rest once a week. Our spiritual, emotional and physical health will benefit.

5. Honour your mother and father. Sounds like saying 'yes' to better family relationships. To expressing love, kindness, appreciation and honour in a world full of dysfunctional relationships.

6. Do not murder (including hate and anger – see Jesus' thoughts on this in Matthew 5:21,22). Say 'yes' to love, kindness and building others up, and 'no' to hate, resentment, gossip and backstabbing.

7. No adultery. That means 'yes' to being entranced with, and focused on real love, and a commitment to living faithfully. It's a 'yes' to investing in your marriage for growth, knowing that the more love you invest (in a whole variety of ways) in your partner, the better the returns, because, unlike some worldly investments, the bank of God (He invented love and marriage) gives positive returns.

8. Do not steal. Say 'yes' to honesty, and giving generously instead, (Ephesians 4:28). Say 'yes' to believing that God knows what I need and will provide it. (Matthew 6:8).

9. Do not bear false witness (or lie). That means say 'yes' to telling the truth, being honest, building trust. I think we can all say, what a brilliant and much needed 'yes' commandment that is because we long to be safe and in a place of trust in our homes, relationships, churches, and jobs – indeed in all areas of our lives.

10. No coveting. A tough one maybe in our world where it's so easy to see what others have; and as consumers we are daily incited to have and get more and more. This 'no' is God's 'yes' to the truth that 'Godliness with contentment is great gain.' (1Timothy 6:6), and we can echo back, "Yes it really is great gain."

DAY 303 | The Ten Commandments (Part 2)

So there we go, the ten commandments are in fact very positive because they are all about saying 'yes' to a life lived in the way that our supremely loving heavenly Father knows is the absolute best for us. Can we imagine a world where everyone is gladly keeping these commandments. What a safe and special place that would be, because the keeping of them by everybody would cover just about every aspect of human life.

To those who feel that Jesus was far more positive, and all about love, let's look at how Jesus summed up 'The Ten' into two commandments. He said "Love the Lord your God with all your heart and with all your soul and with all your strength and with all your mind", covering Commandments 1,2 and 3, and then He said, 'love your neighbour as yourself.'" (Luke 10:27), which covers the last six of the Ten, the ones covering my responsibility to behave towards others in the community in a loving way. Commandment number 4 about the Sabbath day, straddles both because it is about making time for God, looking after ourselves, and so being better placed to truly love others as we would ourselves would wish to be loved.

In our 21st century world we now have a code of 'Human Rights'. They are about the right's of each individual to have others treat them in a respectful way. They began as a wonderful antidote to abuse in all its forms and at all levels of society. They grew out of a Christian culture that declared that all human beings are of great value, are equal and are worthy of the respect of all other human beings. These 'Human Rights' are good and remind us that we are part of a global community in which we need to treat others in the way that we ourselves would like to be treated. They cover Jesus' summary of the last seven commandments, but they don't include the first three.

Now the problem is our human nature. We often want to say, "Why can't I do that? I want to." It's called rebellion. It's that selfish child in us all and once humankind loses sight of, and denies, their Creator, to honour and worship Him, they become intrinsically selfish. (See Romans 1:21-32). With the rejection of the first three Commandments at the same time as the adoption of Human Rights, a significant emphasis in society can shift from everyone being responsible before God to love and treat others (my neighbour in Jesus' terms) as they they would like to be treated, towards a tendency to monitor the behaviour of 'others' towards me. In this way our 'rights' can be elevated above our human responsibilities, 'my' individual rights above the call to serve God in caring for others. And so it becomes harder to guard my heart from offence because I have to stand up for 'me' as I become increasingly aware of what others have, or haven't, done to, or for, me. This can then slip into an expectation that everyone else should be looking after me. We therefore have lowered resistance to the whispers of the enemy that, 'Someone should be doing something about my situation', when the biblical encouragement is first and foremost to 'Trust in the Lord with all your heart and lean not to your own understanding . . .' (Proverbs 3:5,6).

Within the church itself, where we have rightly emphasised the love and goodness of God and the power of God to heal and intervene on our behalf, we can likewise feel 'entitled' and 'take offence' when it feels like God hasn't delivered, or directed one of His children to treat me as I should be treated. We can often miss the fact that there is a need to humble ourselves under His mighty hand, as Job did in the end, when his indignation with God turned to repentance. "My ears had heard of you but now my eyes have seen you. Therefore I despise myself and repent in dust and ashes." (Job 42:5,6). (See also James 4:5-11)

Activation . . .

It's a big topic – Thankfully we have a wonderfully wise Holy Spirit to illuminate us as we consider it. So today thank God for His commandments. Let it dawn on you afresh that these commandments flow from the heart of a very wise Father who loves us to bits and knows what's best for us. Let thanksgiving draw you forward, with hope, into all the best that the Lord has for you. Give thanks for His love and care, His wisdom and desire for your best and 'see' the huge 'Yes' flowing from His heart towards you. First and foremost look to 'love the Lord your God with all your heart mind soul and strength' then you can love your neighbor as yourself and bless others with a free heart, as you let His love care and protection flow towards you.

DAY 304 | Thanksgiving and Saying 'No'

Over the past two days we have reflected on how the ten commandments help us to say a gigantic 'Yes' to God's very best for happy, healthy lives. We discovered afresh that saying 'No' to things that have negative effects on us is a huge 'Yes' to a good life. Remember Jesus said He came that we might "have life, and have *it* abundantly." (John 10:10, NASB). On Day 216 in Book 3 we also observed that saying 'No' to some things that aren't necessarily bad in themselves can help us to reduce the stress in our lives. That stress that comes from over committing ourselves and so I was intrigued recently to read a quote from Warren Buffet, a very successful financier.

The quote was this. "The difference between successful people and really successful people is that really successful people say no to almost everything."[1] Wow! that is something to think about isn't it? Stops you in your tracks a bit! Even if his comment was mainly about business sense and making investments, it can have much wider implications. I think it can probably also apply to the quality of 'success' that we have in our spiritual and emotional lives too.

Now we may ask, "Did Jesus say 'No'? Surely He was always saying 'Yes'?" Well if you mean that His arms were wide open in compassionate invitation to those who were hungry for His love and care, then yes, He was always saying a big 'Yes', but how about his behaviour as described in Mark 1:32-39. There has been a massive time of healing and deliverance with the whole city of Capernaum at His door then, early the very next morning Simon Peter finds Him praying in a solitary place,. "Everyone is looking for you" (i.e. let's get building on this revival here). Jesus' reply is "Let us go somewhere else-to the nearby villages-so I can preach there also. That is why I have come." In effect He was saying "No!" And He did, He moved on to the next village and the next and the next.

Remember that just as every 'No' in the Commandments carries a 'Yes' for our lives, so every 'Yes' also carries a 'No'. So for Jesus, 'Yes' to a longer mission in Capernaum, 'Yes' to pleasing the people there, 'Yes' to continuing with the very visible success in healing and deliverance there, 'Yes' to peer pressure from Peter, all looked attractive, even spiritual, but that 'Yes' would also be a 'No' to all the other people throughout Galilee who needed His message and His power. It would be a 'No' to the purpose for which He had come; perhaps even a 'No' to what His Father had been talking to Him about in their conversation that morning.

The article on successful people saying 'No', gave some further thoughts that resonated with Jesus' behaviour in the gospels. For example we need to say 'No' to things that don't speak to our values or mission in life. Jesus did that. We need to say 'No' to doing it all ourselves – 'Yes' to delegation – Jesus did that, (even though the disciples often made mistakes!) We need to say 'No' to people pleasing; letting other people set the agenda for our lives – Jesus did that too. And then there is saying 'No' to superficial, critical negative atmospheres, instead saying 'Yes' to building relationships, and working with people who are hungry for better things. We don't always have a free choice with that in our work circumstances, but it can still be an important pointer for the rest of life.

So where does thanksgiving come into this equation? Well first let's note again that Jesus said 'No' to Peter, the revival and all the people in Capernaum after time spent in prayer with His Father. I think it very likely that there was thanksgiving in that mix of loving, intimate communion. In our very busy lives, with demands all around, calling for us to say 'Yes' many times a day, stopping to give thanks helps us to tune back in with the Lord. This is so vital. The Lord Jesus, the Son of God did it, so I think that means that I definitely, definitely need to.

Activation . . .

Today, let 'Thanksgiving' reconnect your busy brain with the will of God, (1 Thessalonians 5:18). Let 'Giving Thanks' calm your emotions and bring you back to a more balanced, godly perspective on your life and priorities. Let 'Thanksgiving', re-orientate your spirit, heart and mind to the Lord, His word, His purposes and His priorities for your life, so that they become louder than the noisy demands all around you. Let thanksgiving strengthen your confidence to say 'No', when you need to, without guilt, and so let it bring rest to your soul as you learn from Him. (See Matthew 11:29).

DAY 305 | Thanksgiving that 'Guards My heart'

We continue today with our thoughts around the guarding of our hearts with the weapon of 'giving thanks in all things'. This meditation may, I believe, be the most important of all the days in these four books on thanksgiving because, as I have been praying for those I know who are struggling to hold onto faith, or who have lost faith, I have become aware of how in each case there has been 'offence'. I am aware that very often people have allowed themselves to become 'offended' which has then led to the harbouring of a 'spirit of offence'. Partnering with a 'spirit of offence' will inevitably separate us from the Lord. Guarding our hearts therefore from 'taking offence' is I believe crucial to our spiritual wellbeing.

Now we have written previously about how Jesus encouraged John the Baptist not to get offended when He, Jesus, did nothing to get him out of prison. Jesus sent John a message saying in effect, 'Yes I am the Messiah and all these miracles are happening and yes you're in prison but this is not a time for me to 'set the captive free' for you in your life now. He then finished His message to John with the words, "Blessed is he who takes no offence at me." The point is offence is taken when someone does, or says, something we think they shouldn't have said or done, or doesn't do, or say, something we think they should have said or done. And it happens so quickly, almost imperceptibly, unless we guard our heart very diligently.

Just think how easy is it to get offended by family members, neighbours, the government, work colleagues, our parents, those in our church, or in the church we have left because we were offended. And of course we can also get offended with God who we feel hasn't kept a promise, or hasn't done what we wanted Him to do. And we are particularly vulnerable to 'taking offence' when, like John the Baptist, we are suffering in some way.

Suffering we are told will either make us 'bitter' or 'better'; perhaps the 'I' in 'bitter' stands for the 'I' who is offended. "I will handle this in my way." While the 'E' in 'better' can stand for the Everlasting Father of Isaiah 9:6 in whose hands I can choose to 'rest my case'. In his book The Problem of Pain, C.S Lewis wrote, 'God whispers to us in our pleasures, speaks in our conscience, but shouts in our pains: it is his megaphone to rouse a deaf world.'[1] This does not automatically mean that if we are suffering in some way we have therefore brought that problem and suffering on ourselves, or that God has caused the suffering in order to get our attention.

We do however need to have a theology of suffering; an understanding of suffering from God's perspective, if we are to avoid 'taking offence'. God does not cause suffering and sickness. Suffering and pain were not there before the fall (Genesis 1-3) and they will not be there in heaven (Revelation 21:4). God is good and sent Jesus to destroy the work of the devil, but God may, as He did with Job, allow suffering and will without doubt, as with Job, use suffering in our lives. Job himself having spent a considerable amount of time trying to take God on, declares to Him at the end, "I know you can do all things; no plan of yours can be thwarted." "My ears had heard of you but now my eyes have seen you." (Job 42:2-5)

I may be partly, or wholly, to blame for my difficulties and suffering, others in the world, or the church, may be the cause, the circumstances of the world may be the cause, or even natural disasters. My job is to 'guard my heart' against taking offence over someone else's behavior, Christian, non Christian, government, family member, at work, or in the neighbourhood etc. etc. Why? Because, do you know what? Taking offence will do absolutely no good to anyone, least of all myself. It won't change anything, but it will savage my heart and separate it from God. Now this is not to say, that we never speak up, put in good boundaries, or walk away from difficult people and situations, but in all these scenarios, first of all 'Give Thanks', then you will see the way of deliverance. (Psalm 50:23).

Activation ...

ANY TIME that offense is crouching at your door, consider Cain and Abel, (Genesis 4:1- 15, especially verses 5-7.) and thank God that He loves you and is for you. Thank Him that He will work in this and every situation for your good in His incredible and loving and powerful way, and in His time.

Thank God that He is with you and will spread a table before you in the presence of your enemies. (Psalm 23:5) Incredible! How wonderful is that?

And thank Him that, through it all, as you welcome Him – by your thanksgiving – into the situation, He will be changing you and conforming you into the likeness of His Son. Thank God **in everything and in every situation**, and you will find Him to be faithfully with you in everything.

DAY 306 | Gratitude for my 'Shoes of Peace'

Shoes are fun and functional! I know lots of people just love buying shoes, for others of us it is just a chore, and as long as we have shoes on our feet we don't go looking for more. So I have never quite 'got' the significance of us having our 'feet fitted with the readiness that comes from the gospel of peace.' (Ephesians 6:15). Why did the Holy Spirit singled out our feet in this way, surely sharing the gospel is about what is on our hearts and in our mouths?

Then I got to thinking again. Although today many people tend to wear trainers whatever they are doing, generally speaking, shoes signify what we are about to do. As a child I just loved my ballet shoes, but never had any tap shoes . . . didn't want to go to tap dancing class! If I'm putting on my boots, the dog knows it's time for a walk in the woods, and when we were in Finland, we didn't put on snow shoes until we were in the snow. (N.B. It's just impossible to get up when you fall over in snow shoes – makes you realise how important it is to be able to bend your foot at the toes!!!)

Shoes speak of the business that we are about, so putting a 'readiness to share the gospel of peace' on our feet, gives notice to the enemy of what we are about. We are under orders from our 'Prince of Peace' to be prepared, even eager, to bring His peace wherever we go. Now that is intriguing, when we also hear Jesus asking the question, "Do you think that I have come to bring peace on the earth? No, I tell you, but division." And then He describes a family divided against itself, numerically and generationally. (Luke 12:51-53). I think that Jesus was signaling that the peace He brings is not 'peace at any price', and so we should not be surprised that some may not want to pay the price for the peace that He brings.

So what of us? What are we meant to be doing with our feet shod with the readiness to share 'gospel of peace' in this way? I think He is primarily asking us, in speaking 'peace' to people, to draw them into a place where they can find lasting 'peace with God' through the Gospel. So when Jesus sent out the seventy He gave them specific instructions, 'When you enter a house, **first** say,

"Peace to this house." If a man of peace is there, your peace will rest on him; if not, it will return to you.' He then gives them instructions about eating with those who receive that peace, about healing their sick and then sharing with them that, "The Kingdom of God is near." That is to say let them know that the peace and healing come from Jesus. It's what He does. (Luke 10:6-11).

At the same time Jesus also gave them instructions about leaving a place that did not receive this message of peace and healing. So Jesus knows that, in spite of the fact that the Gospel is such incredibly good news, we are not going to be welcomed everywhere. Nevertheless, our start point is always to go to people with a heart to bless and impart peace. I like that! It gives me confidence that when I talk to someone about the Lord, I am carrying God's peace, and so I therefore have something wonderful to offer them, 'Peace with God'.

It was the message that the angels brought to those first shepherds, "Glory to God in the highest, and on earth peace to men on whom His favour rests." (Luke 2:10,14). Those shepherds responded so quickly and got so blessed, and that's how I want to share the good news with people, letting them know that God wants to give them 'peace', and that peace with God will bring them great joy. My part is to 'offer' that peace, recognising that it may or may not be received, but if **I'm** thrilled about it, and not embarrassed, then surely **others** might become curious and want to know more.

A while ago now, when feeling that I wasn't doing much in the way of sharing of my faith, I felt that the Lord encouraged me that it could be fun!! Perhaps we are back to my original thought; may be these 'Gospel shoes' can be shoes that are functional **and** fun! I think that for me, thanking God that I have 'good news', 'tidings of great joy', and that my feet are 'fitted with the readiness that comes from the gospel of peace' helps me to become ever more confident to share my faith, with joy in my heart, in an increasingly hostile world. Then I can leave the outcome with the Lord.

Activation . . .

Give thanks today every time there is an opportunity to share the good news of God's love with someone. Let your thanksgiving bring you to a place of boldness and confidence that you are going to bring someone some hope and peace in an unpredictably turbulent world.

DAY 307 | Thanksgiving for Beautiful Feet

Yesterday we were considering how, with our 'feet fitted with the readiness that comes from the gospel of peace.' (Ephesians 6:15), we could bring good news to people with confidence, and even have some fun doing so. This is because the gospel is such good news especially to the 'poor, the brokenhearted, the captives, the prisoners and all who mourn'. That is quite a list, and it comes of course, from Isaiah 61:1-3. It was the passage Jesus read out in the temple at the start of His ministry. (Luke 4:18,19). Simply put, the 'Good News' is only going to be 'Good' if someone realises that they have need of Jesus, of His mercy and forgiveness, and His healing and help.

Jesus emphasised this truth when He told the Pharisees, "It is not the healthy who need a doctor, but the sick. I have not come to call the righteous, but sinners." (Mark 2:17). And I wonder if this is why, in our very affluent society where so much is provided for us in so many areas of life, that there seems to be so little hunger for our 'Good News'. Even Jesus, in an occupied country where there was great need, was rejected by the self sufficient. Jesus 'wept over Jerusalem', saying "If you, even you, had only known on this day what would bring you peace – but now it is hidden from your eyes..." (Luke 19:41). Those who felt their need came and found 'peace', while the leaders turned it down, and so He let them know that very hard times were ahead.

It seems important therefore at this time that we, God's people, have our feet well fitted out with readiness to share some Good News when there are so many potentially threatening things on the horizon. We in the west have lived for a long time now with increasing affluence and wellbeing in all areas of life. There is a mentality that things should always get better and better and we change our leadership regularly, voting in those who offer us the best life possible.

Now, however, this generation is facing possible future pandemics, global warming, cyber warfare, the rise of powerful dictators, and the spread of A.I. – all things beyond the power of our government to control. Then we have the more immediate concerns for us here in the U.K. like the potential breakdown in our health service, our social care system, our schools and our economy, with all the implications for social order and cohesion. Not surprisingly people are increasingly feeling that the familiar things that have given a feeling of security, for many years now, are being shaken.

We read, "How beautiful on the mountains are the feet of those who bring good news, who proclaim peace, who bring good tidings, who proclaim salvation, who say to Zion "Your God Reigns!"(Isaiah 52:7). These verses are of course addressed to God's people, and sometimes we need to put on our 'shoes' in order to encourage, first and foremost, our brothers and sisters so that, whatever is happening in the world around us we, God's own people, can still declare, "Our God Reigns."

As the world gets increasingly shaken up by physical, economic, political and spiritual crises, it is going to be very important that God's people are not shaken. If we confidently know that 'Our God Reigns', we can stay steady and continue to offer hope to those around us. God has said, "Once more I will shake not only the earth but also the heavens." . . . so that what cannot be shaken may remain. Therefore since we are receiving a kingdom that cannot be shaken, let us **be thankful and so worship God . . .'** (Hebrews 12:26-28).

'He reigns', and He will be with us in everything, so that we will not be shaken. If we know this we will have a stronger and stronger message for those in the world around us. We want them to see, and therefore be hungry, for what we have in our lives – for our 'Good News'. We want to be those with 'beautiful feet', so that when that time comes and 'Men will faint from terror, apprehensive of what is coming on the world,' when 'the heavenly bodies will be shaken.' (Luke 21:26), we will be seen – 'the sons of God revealed' (Romans 8:19) – as those carrying good news, proclaiming peace and salvation.

Activation . . .

Whatever 'shakings' are happening for you in your life at the moment, thank God and grow in your faith as you prove His faithfulness time and time again in today's challenges. 'Therefore, since we are receiving a kingdom that cannot be shaken, **let us be thankful, and so worship God acceptably with reverence and awe . . .'**. (Hebrews 12:26-28).

DAY 308 | Thanksgiving and Joy

Following on from yesterdays thoughts about the beautiful feet of those who bring 'Good News'. I thought today we really need to think about 'Joy'. Good news always brings joy!! In Isaiah's day of course all news came on foot, a runner would be sent to tell of a hard won military victory, of an impending invasion, or of a new King on the throne. It was even the case that a bringer of bad news might himself be punished, but here the bible speaks of the welcome that a bearer of good news would receive.

We don't have 'runners' these days but good news, however it arrives, still brings great joy. We have probably all seen the footage of the V.E. day celebrations in London after the second world war. Great and uncontainable joy at the end of nearly six terrible years of fighting, tragic loss of life, shortages, displacement and so much more. In our own time I'm sure we have all felt great joy at the announcement of a new baby, of a wedding, or even simply the news that our favourite football team won. Joy always accompanies 'good news'!

The passage quoted above from Isaiah 52:7-9 in The Passion Translation reads like this . . . 'What a beautiful sight to behold – the precious feet of the messenger coming over the mountains to announce good news! . . . announcing salvation to Zion and saying "Your Mighty God Reigns". Listen! The watchmen are shouting in triumph! Lifting their voices together they are **singing for joy!** . . . **Burst into joyous songs**, you rubble of Jerusalem! For Yahweh has graciously comforted His people.'

So as I am walking this morning and thinking around 'joy', I am captivated by the sight of a magnificent oak tree in the full glory of its autumn colours. It's beautifully lit up by the sun – absolutely stunning. And I'm thinking, 'No, not joy! Today's meditation has to be about trees!!' And then I remembered that Isaiah went on to prophesy that when the end of the exile came for Israel; when the good news that had been brought to them came about in real time, they would 'go out in joy, and be led forth in peace; the mountains and the hills will burst forth into song . . . and **the trees of the field would clap their hands.**' (Isaiah 55:12).

That tells me that joy needs to have expression; a sound, perhaps a song, a laugh or a shout, even a movement like a dance, a jump, or the wave of a flag. It is almost as if it is in the physical expression of joy, that it is fully released, and fully felt. Keeping quiet is not an option. Jesus knew that. When He came on a donkey into Jerusalem, the Pharisees wanted Jesus to rebuke the people because they were celebrating His arrival by 'joyfully praising God' with loud voices and waving palm branches. Jesus reply was simple 'if they keep quiet, the stones will cry out.' (Luke 19:37-40). Or the trees?

So what of us? I think sometimes we can get too familiar with the truths of the gospel, we can almost take it all for granted – God's unconditional love, His forgiveness, His faithfulness, the 'New Life', that He has given us. He is always good and He is always with us. We are just so richly blessed in so many, many ways; and then there is the miracle of His indwelling presence. Now that is very, very good news, and it's the news that we have to share with others.

When I receive a piece of good news, like long (long) ago hearing that I had passed my exams, or more recently hearing that a grandchild has been safely born, or that this home that we were buying was finally ours, I always thank God, often just in my heart. And so now I am feeling that when I read a piece of good news in the bible, when someone or something reminds me of the incredible wonder of my salvation, of what is now mine 'in Christ', then I need to get a bit excited and speak or sing out my gratitude.

Activation . . .

We used to sing a chorus that went, 'If you want joy you must sing for it . . . shout for it....jump for it... dance for it etc . . . the joy of the Lord is your strength.' I was never quite convinced!! But now I am beginning to think that I understand it a bit more. Today give voice to your gratitude and see where it leads next. Find a truth or a promise in the bible and let rip with your gratitude. Let your thanksgiving be the entrée to a feast of joy and wonder!!

'Lift up a great shout to the Lord! Go ahead and do it-everyone, everywhere! ... Sing your way into His presence with joy!' (Psalm 100:1, TPT).

DAY 309 | The Releasing Power of Thanksgiving

Psalm 73 is, I believe, a wonderfully helpful Psalm for our lives today, because the Psalmist, like Job, is struggling with life and with some of the conflicts that 'life' is throwing up for him. The psalmist starts off with an honest evaluation of how life often is – God is really good to us, but looking around he is troubled by the pressures, ups and downs, disappointments and battles of life, especially when he sees how well other people are doing; people who, in his estimation, don't deserve to be doing well!

In verses 3 to 14 there is a vivid description, written the best part of 3000 years ago, of how life can sometimes look to us – Christians in the 21st century. Rich people are doing well and prospering, even when their morals and behaviour are suspect. The imaginations of their hearts run riot. There is arrogance and pride. No fear of death or sense of accountability. Casual and self opinionated talk that puts others down and speaks cruelly and judgementally of others. There is no respect or 'fear of the Lord', and in all this they are very comfortable.

Not surprisingly, having sought to walk right with the Lord in heart and life, and willing to accept the Lord's discipline in his life – which is not always comfortable, the Psalmist finds himself troubled and on a slippery slope. But he also realises that if he gives voice to his confusion, pain, bitterness (v21), and perhaps even cynicism and unbelief, he could cause his believing friends to stumble too (v15). He is vexed, distressed and confused – **Until**. What a wonderful word in verse 17. '**Until** I came into the sanctuary of God;' (NASB) And what happens in the sanctuary of God? Thanksgiving, praise and worship.

So what happens then? Well verses 23 -28 give us a good picture. He realises God is so near, He is even holding his right hand. I really like that, especially when I think of one of my grand-daughters holding my hand as we walk along the pavement by the busy, dangerous road. And holding hands isn't just about being safe, it's so warm, close, intimate and belonging. And God never lets go but says "I am continually with you". He is my guide and my strength not just on the good days, but when my flesh and my heart fail. On those days He doesn't say "Buck up." Instead, He is the 'strength of my heart', (v26), where I really need it. And in case I haven't got it yet the Psalmist reminds me that God being very near to me and my refuge is really good for me. (v28).

In the very real lived experience of the Psalmist, an experience that I think nearly every believer can relate to in some seasons of life there is, for me, a very important message. He did not find the initial solution to his pain, confusion, perplexity and bitterness in thinking it through and applying the rational processes that our society and education have emphasised over the last 300 years. Verse 16 says 'when I pondered to understand this, It was troublesome in my sight . . .'. Nor did he feel that a healthy route was just to talk it out, (verse 15, NASB).

I think that it was in worship, praise and thanksgiving in the sanctuary that light came and his eyes, head and emotions cleared. Then he could think, and talk with a God (heavenly) perspective. I think the message here is that **after** thanksgiving and worship have brought me back to the Lord's perspectives things become clearer, and then I can think things through, feeding my mind on God's word and truth. I can also talk, fellowshipping with others; discovering that 'we have the mind of Christ' as we build each other up.

This surely was also Job's experience. We can read 35 chapters where he is trying to think it through, talk with his friends and question God, and no solution. Then four chapters, 38 – 41, of encounter with God and he is (metaphorically at least) flat on his face before God, "now my eyes have seen you." and things are now the right way up and going forward with the Lord big time. I still don't think he understood everything rationally speaking, but he had certainly come into the light spiritually. (Job 42:1-6 and Psalm 36:9)

Activation . . .

Let thanksgiving and worship take you into the sanctuary with the Lord. Encountering Him there time and again is vital when we don't know what God's will is and we are perplexed. Surely this is why Paul indicates in 1 Thessalonians 5:18 that giving thanks in everything is God's will for us. It's first things first. Start off with thanksgiving and worship, and then you will begin to see things from God's perspective and that will renew your peace.

DAY 310 | Thanksgiving and Radiance

If the writer of Psalm 73 tells us that coming into the sanctuary, drawing close to God, is the answer to our perplexities with God's ways, then Psalm 34 tells us that when we do that, when we come close to God, people notice. But let's track back a bit. When we are spiritually troubled, it shows! We can become 'cast down' and this will affect not just our soul (Psalm 42:5,6,11) but our whole demeanor. The Jews would often 'put on sackcloth and ashes' as an outward expression of their sadness but, as I think many of us know, having a 'crestfallen' expression will give it away, regardless of what we are wearing.

Asaph, who wrote Psalm 73, found the answer to his questions and issues with God **when** he "came into the sanctuary of God" (verse 17) a place of thanksgiving, praise and worship. As he drew closer to God in his heart I think his whole demeanor would have changed, and maybe his face would have **shone**. Certainly David, writing and recording his thoughts after his deliverance from Abimelech observes that, 'Those who look to him are **radian**t; their faces are never covered with shame.' (Psalm 34:5). Being close to Jesus, 'the light of the world', causes a change in our expression and it creates **a radiance that reflects His glory.**

John tells us that, 'Through Him all things were made; without Him nothing was made that has been made. In Him was life, and that life was the light of men. **The light shines in the darkness**, but the darkness has not understood it.' (John 1:3-5). Now the darkness might not 'understand' Jesus but for us it is different. As Paul explains, 'For God, who said **"Let light shine out of darkness"**, **made His light to shine in our hearts to give us the light of the knowledge of the glory of God in the face of Christ.**' (2 Corinthians 4:6).

He has **shone** into our hearts, He has drawn us close, and there is no doubt that God's plan is that we ourselves will now **shine** His light into a dark world. Jesus said to His disciples, "... let your light **shine** before men, that they may see your good deeds and praise your Father in heaven.' (Matthew 5:16). And listen to Paul, 'Do everything without complaining or arguing, so that you may become blameless and pure, children of God without fault in the midst of a crooked and depraved generation, in which you **shine like stars in the universe** as you hold out the word of life . . .' (Philippians 2:14,15). We are destined to be 'light emitters' in a dark world!

When we draw close to God, things begin to make sense. 'in your light we see light.' (Psalm 36:9). That may mean that we put to one side our questions, doubts, and issues with God as we choose to worship Him. We can then review those things from God's perspective, letting Him shine His light into our perplexities, and into our hearts, and this then brings His clarity and His truth. Then we can respond to the prophets words 'ARISE, SHINE, for your light has come, and the glory of the Lord rises upon you.' (Isaiah 60:1), as **His 'light' puts a shine on our faces.**

Thanksgiving helps us to keep 'looking at Him', it keeps us focused on all that He is, all that He has done and all that He provides for us, it keeps us **radiating** light into the world. In Psalm 104:15, the psalmist praises God for many things including 'wine that gladdens the heart of man, and **oil to make His face shine**, and bread that sustains his heart.' As New Testament Christians we have the wine of the New Covenant, Jesus' blood paying the price for our forgiveness and Salvation. We have the oil of the Holy Spirit, enabling us to live a completely new life in Christ, **to stay close to Him and so to 'shine'**, and we have bread, God's Word that sustains us day by day.

Activation . . .

Stay very thankful for each one of those incredible blessings and ensure that your face is 'radiant' even in perplexing or trying circumstances when you are tempted to commiserate with those around you. Shine with His radiance and that will ensure that your face is never covered with shame. (Psalm 34:5).

DAY 311 | Thanksgiving and 'Seeing' Myself as God 'Sees' Me!

Have you ever found yourself arguing with God? "No, that's not me Lord." or "No, I couldn't do that!" Well one of the ways in which we can be radiant, and shine for the Lord is by 'seeing' ourselves, now that we are 'new creatures in Christ', in the way that God sees us. Now in case that seems overly self-centered, let us have a look at a couple of people who actually needed to 'see' themselves with all the light that God could give them, and then I think we may realise just how important this 'seeing' can be.

Let's start with Moses. Here we have a man who, having totally messed up in Egypt in his youth, (see Exodus 2:11-15), was not about to raise his hand and rush into volunteering for the huge task of meeting up with Pharaoh – the most powerful ruler in the known world at that time – in order to secure the release of his people from slavery. God however 'sees' him very differently to how he sees himself!

Moses protests to God four times that He has got the wrong man. The protests range from, "Who am I to do this?" to "Who are you? Who is it who is sending me? I don't know enough about you to do this for you." on to "What if the Israelites won't believe me?" (Fair question given that he hadn't been home for a very long time), and then finally, "I'm not very good with words. Please send someone else." (Exodus 3:11-4:13). The problem was that Moses was not 'seeing' what God was seeing, and because of that he nearly missed his life's calling and destiny.

Moses had been miraculously saved from certain death just after his birth. His sister and his mother's plan worked and so he was not just saved but he was positioned and trained for greatness in Pharaoh's own palace. (Exodus 1:8-2:10). His mother, who was then called upon to be his nurse, must have told him that he was one of God's people. When he takes it upon himself to defend one of his own from the Egyptian slave driver, (Exodus 2:11-21) he is in big trouble and so he has to run away,

After many years in the wilderness, shepherding his father-in-law, Jethro's, sheep he gets this 'call' from God who appears to him in the burning bush.

(Exodus 3:1-10) and his excuses begin! God persist with him, and so he relents and goes to Pharaoh with His brother Aaron, and the rest is history. He becomes one of the greatest leaders in the history of the Jewish people, and even appears with Jesus on the Mount of Transfiguration. (Mark 9:2-12).

And what about Gideon? An angel comes to him (while he is in hiding) and addresses him as a 'mighty warrior' and one whom the Lord is with. (Judges 6:11,12). So Gideon starts his conversation with the Lord by informing Him that he himself is, "the least in my family". He also reminds God that his family is, by the way, the "weakest in Manasseh." (Judges 6:15). He only gains his courage to do what he is being called to do when the Lord takes him to hear what the Midianites are saying about him.

What he hears is a Midianite interpreting a friend's dream. He hears him saying, "This can be nothing other than the sword of Gideon son of Joash, the Israelite. God has given the Midianites and the whole camp into his hands." Now 'seeing' it all – and himself – God's way, Gideon rushes back home, galvanizes his troops and, crying "Watch me . . . Follow my lead", he leads them into a miraculous victory. He became the 'Mighty Warrior' that God had 'seen' and called him to be. It's well worth a read. (Judges 7:7-25).

And what of us? If we are going to live our 'new life in Christ' the way that the Lord wants us to; if we are going to be radiant and shine God's light into this dark world, we need to 'see' ourselves the way He now sees us. That means <u>we aren't allowed to write ourselves off, or put ourselves down</u>. We need to 'agree' with what God says about us. This leads to faith, not arrogance or pride, because we know that all that we now are, and all that we are becoming, is because of His grace, favour and presence in our lives.

Activation . . .

Next time God calls you to do something however big (or small but challenging) don't let the size of the task, the size of the obstacles that you see, your skill set, age, or even the size of past failures determine how you view yourself or your ability to do what He asks. Live thanking God, for how **He** sees you and what **He** thinks you can do by His grace. Seal your agreement with Him by the giving of thanks and release the faith to follow Him wherever He leads.

DAY 312 | Thanksgiving and 'Seeing' Myself as God 'Sees' Me! (Part 2)

Today as we continue to look at this subject of 'seeing' myself through God's eyes we are going to contrast two men, Joshua and Caleb, with the other ten spies sent by Moses to be the designated 'prospectors' of the land of Canaan. When they came back from their investigation of the Land, Joshua and Caleb said "We should go up and take possession of the land, for we can certainly do it." They knew that God saw them as victors, they believed that they 'could do it', and they did, although because of the unbelief of the children of Israel they had to wait 40 more years before they got to fulfil that call on their lives. (See the Book of Joshua).

The other ten spies, the ones responsible for that 40 year delay, went into the land as spies with Joshua and Caleb, as directed by Moses, and saw both the succulent fruit – the blessings – but also the strength of the enemy who occupied it. They never got to settle in the Promised Land. In fact they died in the wilderness, because, in their own words, "We seemed like grasshoppers in our own eyes, and we looked the same to them." (Numbers 13:17-33). If only they had believed God and encouraged the people to 'see' themselves the way God saw them – His precious people to whom He had promised 'the Land.'

Now let's take a look at King Saul, a man who failed to fulfill his calling because he couldn't grasp the prophetic words over his life and the truth of how God saw him. He didn't question God like Moses and Gideon, (would it have turned out better for him had he done so?) instead he pressed on but clearly didn't fully embrace what was said to him through Samuel and the prophets.

The first suggestion we have that Saul didn't 'see' himself as God saw him is at his coronation! They couldn't find him and the Lord had to tell them prophetically ". . . he has hidden himself among the baggage." (1 Samuel 10:22). Now this was 'an impressive man without equal among the Israelites – a head taller than any of the others.' (1 Samuel 9:1,2), a man of whom

Samuel had publically declared, "Do you see who the Lord has chosen? There is no one like him among all the people." (1 Samuel 10:24).

What a wonderful introduction to the job, yet he still did not have the faith to be the leader that God wanted. When he later messes up, he seems to have forgotten all the prophetic signs around his calling and he confesses to Samuel, "I have sinned. I violated the Lord's command and your instructions. I was afraid of the people and so I gave into them." (1 Samuel 15:24). His view of himself was way too small and so he needed other peoples' approval and that is what led him into trouble.

You may not have had a prophet like Samuel speak over your life, but the Lord speaks words of encouragement to us in many different ways through His word, read, taught and preached, and through many different people. We need to make sure that we are listening for those words that the Lord speaks into our hearts. We need to receive them, write them down and record them. Checking them out with a good friend is a good idea so that we can be sure that the encouragement is coming from the Lord. Then we can thank the Lord for how He 'sees' us and so live, 'by every word that proceeds from His mouth'. (See Matthew 4:4).

Now these words of encouragement don't need to be about big things like leading a nation through the wilderness. Not many of us will ever be called to do that, but listen out for the positive feedback you get when you share a scripture, or have been hospitable; when you have been led to give someone some money or a gift. Hear the Lord's words to you through someone who expresses their appreciation at the clarity with which you explain the scriptures. The point I am making here is that there are many gifting and callings, and the Holy Spirit is very creative in the ways that He affirms us, and in the things for which He affirms us.

Activation . . .

If you can receive God's words to you, however they come, with thanksgiving, it will enable you to walk by His light, and not yours. It will enable you to walk in boldness and confidence as you start 'seeing' yourself as He 'sees' you, causing you to be ever more radiant in our darkening world. After all He knows far better than you the power of the Holy Spirit who is now at work in you. (Ephesians 3:20).

DAY 313 | Thanksgiving and 'Seeing' my Life through God's Eyes

When it comes to 'seeing' ourselves the way that God sees us, there is probably no more important scripture for our generation than Romans 8:31-39. Inspired by the Holy Spirit, Paul declares that in everything that befalls him, trouble, hardship, persecution, famine, nakedness, danger or the sword, he and his fellow Christians are 'more than conquerors through him who loved us.' And he can say that because he is 'convinced that neither death nor life, neither angels nor demons, neither the present nor the future, nor any powers, neither height nor depth, nor anything else in all creation, will be able to separate us from the love of God that is in Christ Jesus our Lord.'

Paul knows that having God's love, having Jesus as Saviour, and having the Holy Spirit indwelling us, trumps anything else that can happen to us, and anything that anyone else, or any spiritual force can throw at us. That is quite some place of confidence and security. He had this incredible sense that he would never be 'underneath' the circumstances. Nor would he just 'survive', but he would come through triumphant in heaven's eyes. He would, 'overwhelmingly conquer through Him who loved us.' (Romans 8:39, NASB)

Contrast that with the cultural atmosphere in which we now live where, because people don't have 'a mighty God' in their life, many people feel as if they are someone else's victim. They might be victims of the bad behavior and the failure of others, or of broken systems; victims of parents, or their lack of education, victims of criminals, of trolls, or simply of people who disagree with them on social media who make them feel bad. There is no longer the recognition that we live in a fallen world, and so when something is wrong, the conclusion is that someone must be to blame, and must be held accountable.

Now the bible tells us that we are to fight for the widow and the orphan, to look out for the poor and hungry. We are sent to heal the sick and visit the prisoners, so I am not saying that we shouldn't fight injustice or evil when we see it. We are never encouraged however, as followers of Jesus, to fight for ourselves as our first priority, or to always blame others for our difficulties, but like Paul, we are to entrust ourselves to our heavenly Father who is 'able to keep us from falling and to present us before His glorious presence without fault and with great joy-' (Jude verse 24).

Our perspective needs to be different to that of those in the world. So if we see things as God does, and we see our circumstances in the 'light of His light' (Psalm 36:9), it will help us not to take on that 'victim spirit', so very prevalent today. Instead, because we know that 'in all things God works for the good of those who love Him . . .' and that He will use all things and everything to 'conform us to the likeness of His Son'. (Romans 8:28,29), we can like James 'Consider it pure joy, . . . whenever we face trials of many kinds'. (James 1:2-4). Crazy I know, and so counter culture, but very powerful, and we can take up this stance because our 'citizenship is now in heaven', (Philippians 3:20), and our spiritual life is therefore of greater significance than our temporal life.

Thanksgiving lifts my gaze to heaven, it takes my gaze off myself, my wounded spirit, or my bad situation, and it stops me from entertaining any victim spirit. Instead thanksgiving helps me, like Paul to say, "Yes. In this situation I will be more than a conqueror, **through Him who loves me**." We have a very dramatic example of this when Stephen was martyred. We are told that rather than protesting his innocence, or calling for justice to be done, 'Stephen full of the Holy Spirit, looked up into heaven and saw the glory of God, and Jesus standing at the right hand of God'. (Acts 7:55).

Activation . . .

Don't wait until something that shocking happens to you, but by giving thanks in all your current circumstances, gain God's perspective on the things that are happening to you in life right now, and build your confidence in your heavenly Shepherd who will always be with you and will spread a table before you 'in the presence' of your enemies . . . and anoint your head with oil.' (Psalm 23:5). N.B. This is not to say that there aren't those times when, like Paul, we take issue with something that is happening to us and assert our rights, (see Acts 16:37-39 and 22:23-30), but if we are giving thanks and seeing things the way God sees them, we will do that with dignity and confidence, and that too will glorify God.

DAY 314 | Thanksgiving and Waiting

I woke up this morning with one or two potentially 'heavy' things weighing on my mind and then, having got my mug of tea, I sat down to watch the sunrise. I knew it was coming because of the light that was beginning to fill the sky, and I knew it was going to be beautiful because there were some clouds positioned ready to catch the sun's rays, as the earth rotated into the east. These clouds were just a dull grey, nothing spectacular, but I watched and waited hoping to see a morning display of God's glory in the heavens.

'The heavens declare the glory of God; the skies proclaim the work of His hands. Day after day they pour forth speech; night after night they display knowledge. There is no speech or language where their voice is not heard. Their voice goes out into all the earth, their words to the ends of the world. (Psalm 19:1-4).

Then slowly it happened. One small sliver of cloud turned gold, then another and another. Then some higher clouds, catching the rays, reflected first a soft dove greyish pink and then a radiant pink. The purples followed and then the whole sky lit up with colour, and all this quite a bit before the sun itself rose. I just felt the Lord there with me this morning. I could almost sense Him saying with delight, "Watch this!" I had a feeling we were enjoying this display together.

At the same time I was listening to a song 'Wait on you'[1] based on Isaiah 40:31, 'those who wait on the Lord, or hope in the Lord, will renew their strength.' It was a simple lesson I know, but sitting there watching the dawn break so gently and slowly reminded me again that in the spiritual, as in the natural world, God moves with His own timings and not mine.

The thing that struck me about the dawn is that you want it to develop slowly. If the sun had come up instantly instead of slowly, it really wouldn't have been such a feast for the eyes. Likewise waiting on the Lord takes time. It can't be rushed!! As I watched and listened this line was repeated several times... **'That's what happens when you wait, stay right there and you get a little stronger, and you get a little stronger...'** It reminded me that the renewal of strength doesn't come instantly but little by little as we 'entwine' our hearts with His. (See the footnote for Psalm 25:5, TPT. It indicates that the Hebrew word 'qavah', commonly translated as 'wait upon the Lord', means to wrap tightly, or to entwine.) Being entwined with the Lord definitely can't be rushed.

Waiting on the Lord to renew our strength is never going to be a quick fix. It's about drawing close to Him and receiving more of God Himself; His love and His grace. There can be a real joy in the process, like watching the dawn slowly breaking, as we wait and let the Holy Spirit renew our strength, physical, emotional and spiritual and replace weariness in any or all of those areas.

A second thing that struck me this morning was that if there had been a clear sky with no clouds, I would not have seen all that beauty. The sun would have appeared in due course without that magnificent display. A similar thing is true of rainbows of course. We need sun, rain and clouds to get a rainbow. The clouds form the screen onto which the rainbow is projected and the darker they are the more stunning and perfect the rainbow.

Sometimes the things that seem like clouds in our lives, things that we don't really want to be there, do in fact provide the backdrop for God to show us His power and His glory, His loving kindness and His faithfulness. We can therefore thank the Lord for those clouds in our lives, because we know that as we do, we will see God's glory reflected in them as He works everything in our lives for good. (Romans 8:28)

Finally, as this song that I was listening to was ending, the singer, in his own words, sings about what he is doing while he is waiting. He sings, "And while I'm waiting I'll be worshipping, and while I'm waiting I'll be praising. Not complaining..." And there we have it again: Worship, Praise, Thanksgiving, these three things are such an important part of 'Waiting' on the Lord. They are how I 'entwine' my heart with His, and they are how I turn those times of 'waiting' into times of refreshing.

Activation...

Today ask the Holy Spirit to teach you how to 'wait on the Lord'. Set aside some time, and maybe listen to some worship. Let your spirit rise above the 'noise' of your life and you will find yourself being refreshed and renewed.

DAY 315 | Thanksgiving and Remembering

In my bible, the heading for Psalm 78 reads, 'God's guidance of His people in spite of their unfaithfulness.' And in its 72 verses the psalmist does indeed detail the unfaithfulness God's people; their sin and rebellion, contrasting it with God's goodness, mercy and faithfulness.' So like quite a few psalms it has important things to say to us about our life and walk with the Lord.

One of those important things comes to us through the use of the word 'forgot'. In verse 11 we read, 'They forgot what he had done, the wonders he had shown them.' Which are then listed for us in verses 12-16. The consequences of that forgetfulness are spelt out for us in verses 9 and 10, where we read that, although they were fully equipped (as we are in Christ Jesus) they turned back from battle, forsook God's covenant, and refused to walk in His law.

Verses 17 and 18 add to the misery, as we read that they sinned, rebelled against Him and put Him to the test. Then, as the Psalm progresses we find that when really bad trouble came, they did remember that the Lord was their Rock and Redeemer (verses 35,36). But, even though God was compassionate and forgiving (verses 38,39), it didn't last. So again in verse 42 we find them forgetting, 'They did not remember his power- the day he redeemed them from the oppressor.' but God's continuing, care and goodness is still there and detailed for us in the verses 43 – 55.

Quite often when we sin or make a mistake, or notice the sins and mistakes of others, we say "That is the problem." Well, yes! The sin is the problem, but perhaps we need to ask ourselves, "What came before the sin or mistake?" Maybe it was the 'forgetting' that was the big factor preceding the sin, because forgetting and 'not remembering' can easily lead into wrong thinking, which then gives rise to the kind of behaviour that grieves the Lord.

We can see this played out in the Garden of Eden. Eve apparently forgot how wonderful her friendship with God was, and how He walked with them and fellowshipped with them in the cool of the evening. (Genesis 3:8). It would then appear that she forgot exactly what God had said, and so she wasn't fully believing God's good intentions towards her and His abundant generosity in giving her every other tree to eat and enjoy: And so she fell into Satan's trap. For us, the times when things are not going exactly the way we would really like them to, (as was the case for the Israelites in the wilderness) are the times when we need to rev up our remembering machinery big time, and do our level best not to forget our past deliverances. And one of the very best ways of remembering and not forgetting is of course thanksgiving.

If Eve had been thanking God for all the luscious food He had made available to her in the Garden of Eden, and the great carefree life she was enjoying there with Adam, she might have speedily rejected the Devil's idea that God was denying her something good. (See Genesis 1;28-31, and Genesis 3:4,5). Even more so had she been musing with joy and gratitude on the lovely evening conversations she and Adam had with the Lord, as they walked together in the cool of the day.

Moses clearly understood our human tendency to forget, and the negative consequences of forgetfulness, so much so that he repeated his warning about forgetfulness to God's people three times. (Deuteronomy 4:9, 6:12, 8:11.). David also understood and even exhorted himself to 'Bless the Lord, O my soul and forget not all his benefits-', (Psalm 103:2). Every benefit from the smallest (chocolate hobnobs?) to the greatest (my salvation, eternal life, Christ within me, and so much more). 'Remember the wonders He has done,' (Psalm 105:5), and those daily mercies that we can almost overlook.

Moses and the psalmist both recognised the importance of speaking out God's mighty works, faithfulness, strength and goodness to each other and especially to those younger than us. 'Teach them to your children and their children after them.' (Deuteronomy 4:9), 'O MY people . . . I will open my mouth . . . We will not hide them from their children, but we will tell the next generation the praiseworthy deeds of the Lord, his power and the wonders he has done.' (Psalm78:1-4). Speaking out in this way is the opposite of forgetting, and it also helps others not to forget.

Activation . . .

Thanksgiving, is one of the most practical, powerful and simplest ways of making sure I don't forget all that the Lord has done for me. So today be intentional, proactive, and frequent with your gratitude.

DAY 316 | Thanksgiving that the Lord Loves to be Trusted and even Depended upon!

Yesterday we began to explore Psalm 78, a Psalm which in its 72 verses details God's peoples' unfaithfulness, and rebellion (unhappy reading), as well as His goodness, mercy and faithfulness (happy reading). We looked at how thanksgiving is a really practical way of helping us to remember and not forget. So today we are looking at another important thing that we can find in this psalm. It's in verse 7 and it follows the earlier verses in which the writer exhorts his readers and hearers to listen as he tells of the praise worthy deeds of the Lord, His power and the wonders He has done, as well as His laws and statutes. He encourages them to tell the same to their children. Why? So that they "would put their trust (confidence, NASB) in the Lord, and would not forget His deeds, but would keep His commands."

I believe the order of this verse is important. Notice trust and confidence in the Lord come before obedience. Sometimes we teach that the main thing is to obey the Lord, because we see that the children of Israel went wrong when they disobeyed Him, as do we. This is true, but often we don't recognise that what comes before disobedience is often a lack, or loss, of trust. What makes obedience so much easier therefore is a confident trust in the Lord.

If Eve had really trusted that God had her best in His heart would she have disobeyed Him? Joshua and Caleb trusted that God would deliver the walled cities and giants into their hands (BIG problems) and so they were able to obey. The other 10 spies didn't trust and they didn't obey. Hebrews 4 emphasises the importance of faith and believing (verses 2 and 3) and how the absence of faith itself leads to disobedience (verses 6-11).

I think the Hymn writer got the order right and it wasn't just a matter of getting the rhythm and rhyme right. "Trust and Obey, for there's no other way, to be happy in Jesus, but to trust and obey"[1]; and thanksgiving is such a big help here. Sometimes obeying the Lord seems hard, or risky and I can be fearful, or feel I will lose something or miss out. Sometimes I do need to just override my fear. Feel the fear and go ahead anyway, but if I can feast, with thanksgiving, on the goodness, care and kindness of the Lord, my faith and trust will grow. In this way thanksgiving is likely to make obeying Him flow more freely.

Later in Psalm 78:22 we are told that 'they did not believe God or trust in his deliverance.' And in verses 32 and 33 we see the result of not remembering all God's goodness, provision and deliverances for His people, 'they kept on sinning; in spite of his wonders, they did not believe.' Now it seems to me that God's expressed sadness at this unbelief, communicated through the Psalmist, says that the Lord, unlike many humans, loves to be trusted and loves to be depended upon.

We see this in Jesus' life and He shows us the heart of the Father. He never says, "Don't bother me, I'm busy", or "Stand on your own two feet", or "sort yourself out", or "Buck up you weakling", as many people may. No, He says "Come to me. Learn from me" (Matthew 11:28-39). Especially relevant perhaps, when we are weary, having tried to live our lives for Him in our own strength. Effectively He is saying, "I love being trusted." "I love bringing deliverances to your life."

Hebrews 11 is a hall of fame of 'people of faith' who leant hard on Him, and some of us almost need a brain/spirit 'transplant' to recognise that the Lord loves doing things for His people. He loves us running to Him in trust, like children (Luke 18:17), rather than toughing it out in our own strength. He really is quite different from some of our human models. Consider how excited Jesus got about the centurion (Luke 7:9) and the Canaanite woman (Matthew 15:28). They leaned in hard on Jesus and He was thrilled. He was THRILLED.

Activation . . .

Let us allow thanksgiving to fill up our trust tanks so that, especially in moments of pressure, we increasingly lean in, onto Him, believing in His love, power, ability and faithfulness, and also His desire and PLEASURE to be there big time for us, as we **trust** and put our weight on Him. (Psalm 68:19,20).

DAY 317 | Thanksgiving and My Relationships

I was listening this morning to Charles Wesley's wonderful hymn, 'And can it be?' and I heard again, but as if for the first time, that wonderful line, **He 'emptied Himself of all but love,** and bled for Adam's helpless race'. I felt so moved by that line, and it made me think about how we handle all **our** relationships in life, especially the more challenging ones.

Paul wrote, 'Your attitude should be the same as that of Christ Jesus: Who being in very nature God, did not consider equality with God something to be grasped, but made himself nothing, taking the very nature of a servant, being made in human likeness, And being found in appearance as a man, he humbled himself and became obedient to death – even death on a cross!' (Philippians 2:5-8). I guess I knew the 'truth' that is encapsulated here, and understood about the 'servanthood' of Jesus and the 'laying down of His life'- things that we are called to emulate, in attitude and behavior, but there was something else that I 'saw' this morning through that phrase, **'He emptied Himself of all but Love',** that took some pondering. So what did Jesus empty Himself of?

He emptied Himself of the right to defend Himself, protest His innocence, to justify His actions and words, to argue His case. He emptied Himself of any self importance, any need to be acknowledged, any need for affirmation and honour. He emptied Himself of any right to 'kick back', to call down judgement on His tormentors, or to demand deliverance from their violence. We read that 'He was oppressed and afflicted, yet he did not open his mouth; he was led like a lamb to the slaughter, and as a sheep before her shearers is silent, so he did not open his mouth.' (Isaiah 53:7), and so we see that He also emptied Himself of the need to cry out in complaint.

So the challenge comes; How do I respond in different situations? I remember, many years ago, someone sharing the illustration of a glass of liquid. When that glass is knocked, whatever liquid is inside will spill over. If you knock a glass of apple juice, only apple juice will spill out. Likewise you won't get apple juice spilling out if you knock a glass full of sulphuric acid. The point was simple: When we are 'knocked' by life or, or by other people in our lives, what spills out will be a clear indication of what is inside.

When we are hurt, challenged, or have our nose put out of joint in any way by an accusation, a snub, a criticism, felt or implied, we can find ourselves reacting in our own defence with self justification; with a counter snub, anger, or worse. The reason is that although Christ is in us, we still can resort to our 'old man' behaviours when we are caught out, and the more we give in to the old the less chance we have of reacting from the new.

On the other hand, the more that we are filled with our 'new life', and the more we reckon on the 'old me' being dead, the more, when I am knocked, I will respond with the fruit of the spirit and less with the old works of the flesh. (Galatians 5:19-23). I can ask myself, "Was that completely loving, or was there some self preservation in that?" So what am preserving anyway? If the 'old me' is dead, I am free to react from the 'new me' which is Christ in me, filled with the Holy Spirit. He 'emptied Himself of all but love'. Can I?

Now just a little aside here. This doesn't mean that I am going to bury all my feelings, or that I am avoiding, or denying, what is coming at me. It is also not about becoming a passive doormat but it is about letting His life flow freely through me. Jesus often spoke up and challenged people, but whenever He did it was for the sake of 'the other' not His own. If I, like Jesus, **with the absolutely necessary help of the Holy Spirit**, choose to **'empty myself of all but love'**, then when I am 'knocked' it will be His love and life that 'spills' out.

Activation . . .

When I feel 'jostled' by someone's words or behavior towards me, the natural me will probably tense up ready to defend myself. Or I can, by thanking the Lord for this great opportunity, relax, let His life flow, and stop that reaction. I can thank the Lord that He is in me. I can thank the Lord that I am completely, and unreservedly loved by Him, and that the same loving Holy Spirit is filling me and spilling over in love for the person who is currently 'in my face'.

Thanksgiving helps me to allow His life to flow unexpectedly and freely through my personality. I may even surprise myself at what comes from me in those moments; at what comes from my mouth, my demeanor, and even my actions.

DAY 318 | Thanksgiving and our 'Bottom Line'

I want to have a look at Mary and Martha today. Two beautiful ladies, very different to each other, but both very much loved by the Lord. Mary is renowned for anointing the Lord's feet with her perfume and also for being captivated by Jesus teaching, (John 11:2), Martha for 'opening her home' to Jesus, her serving heart, and for getting a little distracted. (Luke 10:38-42). Jesus clearly loved these two sisters and their brother very much, (John 11:5), and He loved being in their home. And so in the light of their devotion to Jesus, and His enjoyment of their hospitality, it is interesting to observe how these two sisters dealt with their disappointment when He apparently 'let' their brother Lazarus die.

The sisters had specifically sent word to Jesus when Lazarus was sick because they had seen Him heal so many others, but Jesus doesn't come. In fact He deliberately delays His visit and, when He eventually arrives, Lazarus has been dead long enough for the mourners to have gathered. Not only had Jesus let Lazarus die, He wasn't even among the first of the visitors to comfort them. (John 11:1-43). Now because we know the end of the story we can often miss just how painful this all was. To lose a beloved brother, (probably the family breadwinner and covering), was terrible enough, but to be let down by the one friend, who could have prevented the death, must have intensified that grief immensely. Bereavement, hard as it is, can be so much harder when people believe it needn't have happened; that there has been a failure or lack of care.

The first thing we can observe here is that Martha went out to meet Him, Mary stayed at home. I think I can identify with Mary here. Sometimes when we are disappointed; when the Lord seems to have ignored our urgent pleas, we can withdraw, not being quite sure how to connect with Him. He appears not to care as much as we thought He did. But when Jesus asks for Mary to come out to meet Him, she does manage to articulate her pain saying, "Lord, if you had been here, my brother would not have died." Mary's deep pain moved Jesus to weep, even though He knew what He was going to do.

Martha is bolder, she goes out and greets Jesus with a similar rebuke, "Lord, if you had been here, my brother would not have died," but she quickly follows it with a bold statement of faith, "But I know that even now God will give you whatever you ask". Well done Martha! She might have been distracted when He was teaching and she was cooking, but she had clearly observed over time, and clocked it, that whatever Jesus asked the Father to do, would be done. They then talk about resurrection and Martha confesses her belief that Jesus is, "the Christ, the Son of God, who was to come into the world."

So what about us when we feel that the Lord has let us down. It could be a prayer not answered, or a promise not fulfilled in the way, or time, we expected. We can be like Mary and withdraw, nursing our hurt and perhaps even our grievance, or we could be like Martha, boldly sharing our pain with the Lord but then, **confessing our bottom line** to the Lord like this. "This may have happened (or may not have happened) and I don't understand you Lord, but what I do know is that you love me and that..."

David knew this. In Psalm 56 he calls on God for mercy. It's another one of those times when his enemies seem to be winning. He is lamenting his fate with lots of tears (which he would like God to note!!). He then makes a great and bold declaration, 'Then my enemies will turn back in the day when I call; **'this I know, that God is for me.'** ... In God I have put my trust, I shall not be afraid. What can man do to me? Your vows are *binding* upon me, O God; **I will render thank offerings to You.** For You have delivered my soul from death, Indeed my feet from stumbling, So that I may walk before God In the light of the living.' (Psalm 56:8-13 NASB).

Activation . . .

Next time you are perplexed with God, find a truth to thank Him for. Remember with thanksgiving something that He has done for you and who He has been for you in the past. It is like finding a rock of faith, on which you can stand, and it will stop you from slipping further down into doubt, unbelief and even self pity. Find your own 'bottom line' and, with thanksgiving, make your declaration of faith. "God this hasn't happened as I wanted/thought/expected, **but this I know ... and I thank you for ...**" I think you will find at that point, (and it may need some persistence) that your enemies (those negative and unbelieving thoughts in your mind that pull you down) will turn back and, like David, you will be able to 'walk again before God in the light of life'.

DAY 319 | Thanksgiving a Door of Hope

Yesterday we talked about thanking God when we are confused or disappointed by something that has, or has not, happened for us. We reminded ourselves of our 'bottom line'; a truth from God's word about His revealed nature and character, or something from our past walk with God, upon which we can stand and like David say, **"This I know, God is for me."** (Psalm 56:9, NASB). Thanksgiving for that truth in the face of something we had hoped that God would do for us which, as yet, has not come good for us, is a great way to stop our slide into doubt, or even cynicism.

If thanksgiving for that 'bottom line' can stop our fall into unbelief, then thanksgiving for other things from our history with God – our Salvation, things that He has done for us, or times when we have been blessed – can further help to lift us back into a place of faith. Thanksgiving can be a doorway for us into fresh hope. And we know that hope is very important for us. It's the stepping stone into faith, because, 'FAITH is the assurance of things hoped for, the conviction of things not seen.' (Hebrews 11:1, NASB).

We also read however that, 'Hope deferred makes the heart sick' Too much delay and we can feel very bad and robbed of the 'life' that 'a longing fulfilled' brings. (Proverbs 13:12). I have often spoken to those who actually don't want to revive their hopes because of the fear of further disappointment, and that's a tricky one to counter. But the answer probably lies in our understanding of the word 'hope'.

Hoping in God is very different to 'hoping' that the bus will come. It is also very different to 'hoping' for a pay rise; then on the basis of that 'hope', taking out a loan only to find myself financially sunk when it doesn't happen. Hope in the bible is 'sure and certain' because it is based on the character of God, not the efficiency or otherwise of the bus company, or the traffic conditions on a certain day.

Even so 'hope', by definition can be a difficult thing to hold onto because the word implies that this is something that we aren't yet seeing because it is in the future, 'We only hope for what we don't yet see.' (Romans 8:25, NASB), therefore looking for reassurance in our circumstances may be fruitless. Our hope has to depend on who God is, and what He has said.

Now Abraham, the Father of Faith, can give us a lead here. God changes his name from Abram to Abraham when he is ninety. It's a change in meaning from, 'exalted Father' to 'Father of multitudes', but he has no offspring and no earthly hope of having any! But there is the promise that Sarah will have a child, the fulfillment of his hopes. Abraham has to walk round, an old man with this new name, but no child in sight, and that could have been a very challenging time for him amongst his friends and neighbours.

How did he do that? Paul tells us that, 'Against all hope, Abraham in hope believed and so became the father of many nations, just as it had been said to him.' (Romans 4:18.) And how did he manage to do that? Well Abraham 'grew strong *and* was empowered by faith as he gave praise *and* glory to God. Fully satisfied *and* assured that God was able *and* mighty to keep His word *and* do what He had promised.' (Romans 4:20,21, AMP).

He had no circumstantial evidence to support his hope, in fact when he considered his own body, and Sarah's too, the complete opposite was true, but Abraham 'gave glory'- gave thanks – to God for His promise, and probably for his past experienced with God too. Abraham had history with God and I think he would have pulled hard on what he knew of God in order to stand firm in those final ten long years of waiting and hoping for a son.

Activation . . .

Abraham's faith was actually strengthened in the waiting time. So, if you are in a time of waiting, give thanks for what you have already seen in your past with God. Then let your hope turn into faith and let your faith bring you peace. 'And hope does not disappoint, because God has poured out his love into our hearts by the Holy Spirit, whom he has given us.' (Romans 5:5).

Use thanksgiving today to reopen any doors of hope in your life that have been closing because of what feels like God's 'delay'. Let thanksgiving increase your faith as you wait and, 'May the God of all hope fill you with all joy and peace as you trust in him, so that you may overflow with hope by the power of the Holy Spirit,' (Romans 15:13).

DAY 320 | More about that Door of Hope

Yesterday, we looked at how thanksgiving for past blessings and mercies can open a door of hope for us in our 'today's'. A door of hope that can lead us into faith for that which we need, and for those things that we believe God has promised us. We saw how Abraham believed for the impossible, becoming strong in faith, 'as He gave glory to God'. (Romans 4:18-20). Paradoxically his faith grew in the ten years that he had to wait as his body, (and Sarah's) was getting older and older. There was absolutely no circumstantial evidence to support his hopes. His circumstances were, in fact, more likely to confirm his doubts and fears, but thanksgiving kept his eyes on the Lord rather than the material facts of his life.

For us things may be a little different because, unlike Abraham, most of us have probably not had such a clear word of promise from God. Often in our times of waiting and hoping there is also some uncertainty around whether or not we have really heard God aright. Did He really promise us ... ?, and therefore in a time of waiting we can also wonder whether He really wants to give us what we have asked for, and for which we are 'believing.'

For me thanksgiving even in these situations is still the door opener to hope and then faith. If in my uncertainty I can focus on the character of God, and can thank Him for truths like, '... no good thing does he withhold from those whose walk is blameless.' (Psalm 84:11), or 'He who did not spare His own Son, but gave Him up for us all- how will He not also, along with him graciously give us all things.' (Romans 8:32), and 'His divine power has given us all everything we need for life and godliness, through our knowledge of Him who called us by his own grace and glory.' (2 Peter 1:3), then my hope will grow.

"Well those verses are about our 'spiritual' life." I hear you murmur, and yes I would agree, but we can also thank the Lord that He is my 'Jehovah-Rohe', The Lord my Shepherd. He is Jehovah-Jirah, the Lord my Provider, He is 'My Refuge and Strength, (Psalm 46:1), and so on. There are so many truths and promises about God's character and His intention towards us His children in the Bible that we need never be without encouragement from His Word. And remember, our Heavenly Father is not impractical, as Jesus told us "Your heavenly Father already knows your needs". (Matthew 6:32, NLT).

But what if I have got it wrong? What if what I am hoping for, and endeavoring to 'believe for', is not on God's agenda for me? Am I just wasting my time and heading for a great disappointment after all? How long do I hold on 'in faith'? So once again, I come back to 'thanksgiving'. The kind of thanksgiving that will help me to focus on the biggest truths of all; on the rich blessings of having a triune God.

So let's assume that we have got it wrong, or even a bit wrong: That what I am 'hoping for' is not what God is planning to give me or do for me? If I am thanking God Almighty that He is my extremely loving, generous and powerful heavenly Father, He like any good Dad will steer me away from what might not be the best for me. He will renew my mind and turn my gaze towards what is His 'good, pleasing and perfect will.' (Romans 12:1,2).

If I am 'giving thanks' to Jesus His Son, who said, "If you live in me and my words abide in you, ask whatever you will and it will be done for you." (John 15:7), I will be open and able to 'hear' and align myself more accurately with His words and will, so that my asking and believing will be robbed of any soulishness or selfishness. And if I am expressing my gratitude to the Holy Spirit who will lead and guide my praying and, even when I don't know how to pray, will pray for me, in me and through me according to God's will (Romans 8:26,27), then I am not going to be disappointed. He will moreover give me His peace as I partner with Him in this way. (Philippians 4:6,7).

Activation . . .

So it is all about knowing who our God is and how much He loves us. Let us mine His Word for some wonderful truths, upon which we can build our hope and then our faith, as we thank Him for who He is and what He wants to be for us at this time in our lives.

Remember that God proclaimed Himself to be, "The Lord God, the compassionate and gracious God, slow to anger, abounding in love and faithfulness..." (Exodus 34:6). We can certainly thank Him for that, and see that 'door of hope' swing open. He also told Moses, "I AM WHO I AM *and* WHAT I AM, *and* I WILL BE WHAT I WILL BE;" (Exodus 3:14, AMP). So ask Him who He wants to be for you at this moment in your life.

DAY 321 | Thanksgiving and Connection

As I look back over the meditations of the last few days, I am realising afresh that in situations where our faith is challenged, our relationship with the Lord can be put under strain. Staying in a place of 'Thanksgiving' is, at these times, a wonderful way of keeping my heart open to the Lord. It is a way of staying positively connected to Him.

We have, perhaps, all experienced the teenager who goes to their room and shuts the door, effectively breaking off communication with the rest of the family. It's a way of shutting out those with whom they disagree, and a way of registering that disagreement in a very physical way. It's also a way of shutting themselves in with their way of seeing things. It's a way of not having to listen to another point of view with which they don't agree.

Gratitude, as we have flagged up throughout this year, keeps us connected with people in a very positive way. It keeps us open and receptive to them. This is also the case with God, and I believe this is why maintaining a heart of thanksgiving, through all the difficulties and complexities of life, is a profound key to staying connected with Him, particularly when He seems to have a different opinion to me as to what needs to be done!

Another reason for retreating to our room when we are teenagers is to nurse our hurt, it's to stop having to be around those who we feel have hurt us. We can be like that with God too. Sometimes it's easier to feel a little sorry for ourselves, and lock Him out, than to face 'full on' the challenges that life brings our way. At these times thanksgiving helps me to break through that bit of a sulk in which I want to indulge, when I have a clear idea of how He should act on my behalf and I don't think God has quite understood how bad things are, or how much I need Him to come to my rescue in some way or other.

Finally we all know that a sign that someone, teenager or otherwise, is not at ease with us, is that they avoid eye contact. This can be because of their own lack of confidence, shame or self-consciousness, or because there is something that you have said or done that displeases them; something that has put a wall up between you and them.

There can also be a lack of eye contact when a child or teenager is forced to say 'thank you' for something that they really didn't want, and for which they really aren't grateful. A quick cursory 'thank you', while looking elsewhere, or while making a quick escape, is clearly not going to build any relationship with anyone. I was then thinking that, having been on this journey of 'Thanksgiving' now for eleven months, (if you have been reading through Books 1,2 and 3), we can do something very similar to avoiding 'eye contact' with the Lord.

Staying in good connection with the Lord is about making our thanksgiving heartfelt, full faced and with eye contact, not just a cursory mutter, as we slink (metaphorically) off to our room. And here I am thinking of the line from a song I have enjoyed recently. It goes 'From my heart to the heavens, Jesus be the centre...'[1] I want my thanksgiving to be heartfelt, and even if I have to start giving thanks, in a particular situation, as a willful choice, I want my words, thoughts and heart to connect with my Heavenly Father, as the Holy Spirit helps me. This, I believe, is true heart connection with heaven.

Activation...

There are wonderful blessings if we stay in good connection with God. We stay positioned to receive all that He is, His love, grace, power, kindness, patience, faithfulness..., and all that He wants to give us. We are also more likely to gain understanding of His ways, and the wisdom to know what to do. In fact the benefits of staying close are just unending, so the next time that you feel like 'running to your room', instead turn your face towards heaven, give Him 'eye contact', and as the Spirit enables you, give Him 'by faith' your heartfelt thanks.

DAY 322 | Thanksgiving and our Differences

Have you ever found it difficult when a fellow Christian, who seems to be in a good place with God, feels able to do things that you don't feel right about? Or the other way round; you are doing/have done something, or have a view on something, that other Christians feel is wrong. I find Paul's discussion in Romans 14 into 15 very helpful in this respect in a number of ways. It contrasts with the dogmatic positions that we can so easily take, on matters of Christian faith and practice. It seems that there are truths on which we should stand firm and unshakeable, but that there are other areas where we are all on a journey, with Jesus, being changed to be like Him.

So how does thanksgiving help us with this? Well Romans 14:6 gives us a reason to take a long pause for thought. 'He who regards one day as special, does so to the Lord. He who eats meat, eats to the Lord, for he gives thanks to God; and he who abstains, does so to the Lord, and gives thanks to God.' So instead of arguing whether we should or shouldn't eat meat, go shopping on Sunday, wear different clothes to church, have women preach or be bishops, only have ordained people give communion, and many other things on which Christians differ, it seems that Paul is giving us a vital key. Whatever is your current conviction wrap it up, like a tasty M&S tortilla wrap, in a lovely coat of thanksgiving. If you find it hard to freely give thanks from your heart for how you are seeing it, maybe it's time to check it out with the Lord – see verse 22, 'So whatever you believe about these things keep between yourselves and God. Blessed is the one who does not condemn himself by what he approves.'

And with regard to others, this giving of thanks for them is also very important. It can seem counter culture in our more polarised society, where many seem to increasingly believe, speak, write and tweet in not so many words, "I am right and you are wrong and therefore you are bad." But instead of judging my brother or sister, let me thank God for them whatever their political convictions, and even more especially if it concerns a particular aspect of church life or Christian living. Let us seek, as we thank God for each other to gain understanding and bless; to build up and not pull down.

As we thank God in our current position of conscience and conviction, it cuts the legs off our tendency to judge each other, and it puts legs on my desire to honour my brother or sister in his/her current place of conscience and faith. It can also help me not to cause them offence or stumbling in their faith by my actions or words. (verses 13-16).

If verse 23 is true, that 'everything that does not come from faith is sin.' then thanksgiving to the Lord for my current convictions and conscience is a big practical way of walking closely with Him in faith on my journey of being changed one degree at a time to be more like Jesus. Likewise recognising, honouring and being thankful helps me to see that that my brother or sister, who seems to currently have a different position to mine in conscience and convictions, are also walking with Jesus on his or her journey. That doesn't of course mean that I am not open to, and even expecting that, Jesus is changing me and them. But thanksgiving wherever we are all at, changes the atmosphere, feeds faith and makes us more likely to be open to be changed by the Lord than does judgment, – which can frequently be the more natural human response. Thanksgiving creates an atmosphere for us where we can lovingly build each other up in positive fellowship. (Ephesians 4:15,16).

Isn't God clever, wonderful, gracious and mysterious (in a good way), to be able to happily walk with all His children in all their stages of growth, and with all our variety of views, and convictions, that sometimes seem so incompatible? So thank the Lord today that He loves to walk with you and all your different fellow believers too. Thank Him for this amazing holy diversity! He knows what He is doing in each of us, He knows each of our stories, our history and our journey so far. He has not finished with any of us yet, and because of His love and grace, He loves us just the way we are, and He also loves each of us too much to leave us as we are. Thank Him that He is the potter and we are the clay. My task is to surrender to His moulding of me, not to participate arrogantly in the moulding of another.

We are living in times where social media is causing an unprecedented tendancy to replace dialogue and debate with dogmatism. So let thanksgiving enable you, in your dealings with others, to be counter cultural.

'Bear with each other and forgive ... and over all these virtues put on love, which binds them all together in perfect unity. Let the peace of Christ rule in your hearts ... And be thankful.' (Colossians 3:12,13).

DAY 323 | Thanksgiving and Truth

It is so, so difficult these days to know what the truth is about so many things that are happening in our world. To know which part of the news is 'true', which politicians are telling 'the truth', and what is being withheld when we are being fed a particular story in the media or on-line. In addition we now have the post modern dilemma of truth being something that is 'relative to me'. The statement, 'This is my truth' as opposed to 'this is how I see it' is now a valid way of elevating 'my take' on something that has happened, above the understanding of another. It can even be used to put others down, or nullify their understanding of something that has been experienced.

Truth is such an important thing. A common understanding of what truth is, is so necessary for any kind of civilized society to hold together, and therefore a free press giving varied perspectives has always been vital for a democracy to function properly. I now understand a little more why in a court of law, a witness swears to, 'Tell the truth, the whole truth, and nothing but the truth...', because none of us can make accurate judgments if we don't have the true facts of a situation. Pilate had this dilemma at Jesus' trial, when Jesus told him, "Everyone on the side of truth listens to me." Pilate then asked that now famous question, "What is truth?" (John 18:37,38) How wonderful then that we, who belong to the Kingdom of God, have a Saviour who is TRUE; who is described in Revelation as the one who is called 'Faithful and **True**' (Revelation 19:11).

At the beginning of John's Gospel we read 'The Word became flesh and made his dwelling amongst us. We have seen his glory, the glory of the One and Only, who came from the Father, full of grace and **truth**.' (John 1:14). Jesus even calls Himself 'the way the **truth** and the life,' (John 14:6), and He encouraged the young believers, His followers, by saying to them "If you hold to my teaching, you are really my disciples. Then you will know the **truth** and the **truth** will set you free." (John 8:31,32). **Truth** is such an essential part of who our God is, and it is why we can, one hundred per cent, put all our confidence and trust in Him, both for salvation, and for the whole of our lives.

Now contrast the **'trueness'** of our God, with the lying and deceptive nature of the enemy who was, 'a murderer from the beginning, not holding to the truth, for there is no truth in him. When he lies, he speaks his native language, for he is a liar and the father of lies.' (John 8:44). (and of all that is false, AMP). It is in his nature to lie, and therefore his main form of attack is to lie to us. Then by every means at his disposal, he will deceive us into believing those lies. This is probably why Paul, when encouraging us to use all the armour of God, starts by telling us to 'stand firm, with the belt of **truth** buckled around your waist.' (Ephesians 6:14). The belt was of course necessary to hold other parts of the armour in place, especially the breastplate and the sword.

If I don't protect myself from the enemy's lies about the all sufficiency of Christ's death and resurrection, then my breastplate of righteousness may have a few holes in it, making me vulnerable to accusation and condemnation. I may even resort to working hard to gain forgiveness, (yet again!) And if I don't grasp the fundamental truths of God's word, my sword will probably be a bit blunt, and I will lose my 'cutting edge' in any situation of warfare.

I do believe, (as I am sure you do by now), that keeping my heart filled with thanksgiving for all the truths I now know from God's word, will guard me against any confusion that the enemy will try to bring into my heart and mind, particularly about my faith in God's character, His goodness and faithfulness. Keeping my heart filled with thanksgiving, for God's 'truths', is a powerful antidote to any lies that the enemy brings to me. If my heart is full of gratitude, his lies will 'jar', but the truth that the Holy Spirit brings to me will resonate with my spirit, bringing peace and freedom. This is because He is 'the Spirit of **truth**', who comes, 'to guide us into all **truth**.' (John 16:12).

Activation . . .

So today thank God that He embodies **'truth'**, that He is **true,** and therefore totally trustworthy. Thank Him that His written word is **'truth'**. And thank Him that you have the Spirit of **truth** living within so that you can walk in His **truth,** and be protected from the lies of the evil one, as you discern those lies and half truths when they assault your mind. As and when you recognise them you can reject them, refusing to partner with them. Instead you can replace them with **'the truth'** that the Holy Spirit brings to mind: **Truth** that God has already spoken in His Word.

DAY 324 | Appointed to Give Thanks

A friend recently brought to my attention two people in the bible about whom very little is known, but who I believe are very significant for us as we come towards the end of our year of 'Thanksgiving'. They are found in 1 Chronicles 16:41 and they are called Heman and Jeduthan. They, with others, were **'chosen and designated by name to give thanks to the Lord, "for His love endures forever."'** So I got to wondering why it was that, among the priesthood, a few men were named and designated for this specific task. Why, when there were so many important ceremonies and rituals in place, did this little group get commissioned in this way?

As I pondered this question, I began to think that, maybe, it was so that they could be undistracted in their task of keeping the direction of their thoughts towards, and so their connection with, God by their thanksgiving. They would stay true to the task in whatever state the nation found itself. It would only take a small dedicated number to keep the focus on the Lord's enduring love, and to speak, sing, or shout that out. This would turn the gaze of all the priests, and then all the nation to the faithfulness of their God. They were to be a small dedicated and designated group setting the spiritual direction of the nation.

This would be true in times of war, in times of political unrest, and in times of famine or drought: All those times, in fact, when others would be focusing on things like battle plans, resources and survival, or combating false religions. They would be a small, but dedicated, band who were keeping their hearts in gratitude and worship, thereby reminding everyone from where the needed help was going to come. (Psalm 121:2). Their thanksgiving for the Lord's steadfast love would also be needed in times of prosperity and rest, for God knew that this was often a dangerous time when His people could forget Him and all that He had done for them. (Deuteronomy 4:9, Psalm 103:1-5).

It occurred to me that, in a similar way, when we are assailed by things that would distract us from the Lord's goodness; the physical challenges of life like our health, our finances, where we live, etc.; or the emotional ones – our relationships, our job situation, our losses and bereavements; or even the spiritual ones, 'Where is God in this situation?', 'How am I going to cope?', 'What is the right thing to do in this situation?' 'Why is this happening now?', then we need a small, but significant, part of us that will settle our focus on the Lord. A small part of us to keep our connection with the Lord strong; a small, but powerful, part of us that will draw the rest of us – body, emotions, mind and spirit in the right direction.

So what might the small 'named and designated' part of me be? Well how about, 'O Lord, **open my lips**, and my mouth will declare your praise.' (Psalm 51:15)? Or, 'Because your love is better than life, **my lips** will glorify you.' (Psalm 63:3), and 'May **my lips** overflow with praise, for you teach me your decrees.' (Psalm 119:171). Perhaps the writer to the Hebrews sums it up writing, '... let us continually offer up a sacrifice of praise to God, that is, the fruit **of lips that give thanks** to His name.' (Hebrews 13:15, NASB).

It's not literally the same part of our anatomy, but I think James captures a similar thought when he reminds us of the power of the tongue. In this letter he describes how a 'small rudder' can steer a big ship, or a small spark can set a forest ablaze. Lips, mouth, tongue, they are all small parts of the body, but with such power. If praise and thanks are coming from our lips as sweet water, other less pleasant things won't! (James 3:1-12). No wonder the Psalmist wrote, 'Set a guard over my mouth, O Lord; keep watch over the door of my lips.' (Psalm 141:3).

When we talk about someone giving 'lip service' to something we feel that perhaps they are not being very sincere. Now Jesus was clear, He did not want words alone. He spoke with sadness of those who, "honour me with their lips but their heart is far from me." (Matthew 15:8). So we are not talking about using our lips in mindless thanksgiving by rote. Let us instead make sure that our heart 'follows' the words leaving our lips, so that we glorify Him with our thoughts and spirits too.

Activation ...

Today **designate** and **dedicate** your lips for thanksgiving. **Set your lips to 'serve' you,** as the 'member' of your body that leads your mind, emotions and spirit. Let your lips help you at all times to keep your focus on the Lord's goodness as you use them to continually give thanks at all times. (Psalm 34:1).

DAY 325 | Give Thanks, Worship and Prophesy

I love the thought, that some of us, like Heman and Jeduthan, could be chosen and designated by name to be 'thanks givers' in the body of Christ. In Ephesians 4:11,12, we are told that we have prophets in the body of Christ who in addition to 'prophesying' also have the task of provoking all of us to use that gift, so that 'all may prophesy'. (See 1 Corinthians 14:1,31). We have evangelists, those gifted in bringing others to Christ, who also have the role of provoking the rest of us to live evangelistically. (1 Peter 3:15). So in the same way, every child of God needs to be giving thanks on a regular basis, but maybe there are some in the body of Christ who are designated by name for this joyful task, and whose job it is to provoke others to give thanks also.

Now should that seem like a very narrow remit, let us look a little closer at one or two other things that we know about Heman from 1 Chronicles 15:16-19. We read there that he was among those who were appointed to sing joyful songs and to play musical instruments. Heman himself was to be found sounding the bronze cymbals. There is no doubt that designated 'thanksgivers' will also be worshippers, to be found among those who make a joyful sound because, as we know, 'thanksgiving' feeds the heart of worship, and takes us quickly into God's presence. (Psalm 100:4).

We can also note (1 Chronicles 25:5) that Heman is described as the Kings seer, someone with a prophetic gift. This may have come from his grandfather Samuel, (1 Chronicles 6:33), but it would also I'm sure be linked to his designated task of 'Giving Thanks'. If, as we have said, giving thanks is a wonderful means of staying closely connected to our wonderful Heavenly Father then it is also, I believe, going to enable us to hear His heart and speak it out with confidence. We are encouraged by Paul to 'eagerly desire spiritual gifts, especially the gift of prophecy... everyone who prophesies speaks to men for their strengthening, encouragement and comfort.' (1 Corinthians 14:1,3). We should also, 'try to excel in the gifts that build up the church'. (1 Corinthians 14:12).

The gift of New Testament prophesy may be different to the 'office' of a 'seer', or prophet, in the Old Testament, but it is the same Spirit and the same God who wants to speak. So there we have it, if you want to be an encourager, someone who hears from God and builds up brothers and sisters with 'words' from the Lord, you are more likely to be available and ready to do this if you are in a place of thanksgiving. Thanksgiving both to God, for who He is and what He does, but also in thanksgiving for the brother or sister there in front of you, who you are seeking to bless and build up.

One further reference to Heman comes in 2 Chronicles 5:12-14. It's that wonderful passage telling us what happened when the Temple was finished and the Ark of the Covenant was brought in and placed in 'the Holy Place'. The priests withdrew from 'the Holy Place' and all the Levites who were musicians, including Heman, played their instruments and stood, 'with one voice, to give praise and thanks to the Lord. . . . they raised their voices in praise to the Lord and sang, "He is good; His love endures forever." And as they did so, the presence of the Lord came. The glory of the Lord came as a cloud and filled the Temple. The priests, we are told, were overwhelmed by the glory of God, and could no longer 'perform their services'.

Thanksgiving is so powerful, it leads us into worship and into God's presence. It also helps us to grow in the prophetic, by enabling us to hear God's heart and to release His words of encouragement to others. It can also play a huge part in welcoming and therefore releasing the presence of God into our gatherings.

Activation . . .

Today wherever you are and whatever you are doing, make thanksgiving a priority. Be a designated 'Giver of Thanks' and notice how you become more aware of receiving encouraging words for others.

Then next time you are in a gathering for worship with other believers, don't leave it all to the choir, or worship leaders, give thanks from the bottom of your heart and see how God's presence becomes more real to you. Then have faith that your thanksgiving can significantly bring the blessings of God into that meeting or gathering and the people around. N.B. You don't have to be 'leading' to do this.

DAY 326 | Thanksgiving that brings me back to Simple Foundations

Have you ever noticed how the devil loves to complicate things. He complicated things for Eve in the garden (Genesis 3 1-13). The Pharisees complicated the Law adding many micro-managing additions to it between the time of Malachi and John the Baptist. Then from the early days of the New Testament up until now we, as individual Christians, and as groups in our churches, seem to have got into unhelpful habits of making things complicated. We often tie ourselves in knots and do the same to others. I guess that there is something in our humanity and our pride that can take us that way. Could it be too much eating fruit from the tree of the knowledge of good and evil, rather than the tree of life? Remember that 'Knowledge puffs up, but love builds up.' (1 Corinthians 8:1).

In Luke 10 we read of the time when Jesus sent out 72 of His disciples into the harvest field of Israel. He gives them His authority to go in His name, to heal the sick and then to let those people know that 'The kingdom of God is near you.' (verses 8,9). The disciples come back overjoyed at all that they have seen, and especially at the demonstration of power and authority that Jesus had given them over evil spirits (verse 17). Then in the following verses we read something very important about thanksgiving, rejoicing and our source of joy.

Jesus, after all their success pulls His disciples (male and female – Luke 8:1-3) back to the root and rock on which their joy and thanksgiving should be founded. He says, "However do not rejoice that the spirits submit to you, but rejoice that your names are written in heaven." (Luke 10:20). Or as we might say: "Let's get back to basics, and start by keeping it simple." If our rejoicing is just based on the latest miracle that we have seen, then we are very vulnerable when we go through a barren time or a time of spiritual drought.

Now since we live in the material world it is not surprising that often our thanksgiving is very influenced by what is happening in the now; by what we can see, hear, feel, touch and understand in our physical life, but if we follow Jesus' advice when we are having a bad day and can't think of anything for which we can thank God – we can go back to basics. As Brian Howard's song goes, 'Let us give thanks, that our names are written, written in the book of life, inscribed upon His palms.'[1]

Simply giving thanks for these basic truths can also be a great blessing when it comes to clearing my head from the complexities of life, whether in my day to day life, my relationships, or my spiritual life. Perhaps things in life haven't fallen into place as I think that they should. Maybe difficulties in relationships seem insoluble, or people aren't healed when I pray, and I don't know why. Then what about when doctrines are challenged and I don't have an immediate answer. All these things can vex us, sending us running to the tree of knowledge of good and evil.

So giving thanks that my name is written in heaven can 'steady the ship'. Then after I have feasted on that foundational thanksgiving for a while, there is more I can move on to. I can give thanks that, 'the Lord is good and his love endures forever; his faithfulness continues through all generations.' (Psalm 100:5). That's about giving thanks for God's goodness, love and faithfulness as they have been demonstrated in my daily life. Then I can move on and also be thankful for the authority He has given me, His child, in the spiritual world. The same authority which the disciples had just experienced.

Jesus practiced what He preached, (He did!), because in the following section in Luke10: 21 (NKJV) we read, 'In that hour Jesus rejoiced in Spirit and said, "I thank You, Father, Lord of heaven and earth, that You have hidden these things from *the* wise and prudent, and have revealed them to babes. Even so, Father, for so it seemed good in Your sight"' He thanks Father not for the miracles performed by the disciples but that they had been given wisdom and revelation about Salvation from the heavenly realm.

Activation . . .

Next time you feel a bit foolish, simple or childlike because your internal voice, or someone else, says to you "life is more complicated than that – it's silly or unreal to trust God so simply and be so thankful...", reply to yourself (or the other person), "Well I'm one of the Father's babes on whom He is pouring light, revelation and salvation like Jesus said, and what's more, "my name is written, written in the book of life, inscribed upon His palms."

DAY 327 | The Thanksgiving that is at the Heart of True Christianity

Over the year we have looked at many aspects of thanksgiving; at how it is so important and such a blessing both to God and man, but it is good to to be reminded again just how much this simple act marks out a key difference between true faith and much religious activity. This is because there is a natural tendency in human nature, and therefore in much religious activity, towards working hard and doing the right things to please God/the gods as the primary way to keep Him/them happy and receive His/their blessing.

We read however in John 1:12 that, 'to all who **received** him, to those who believed in his name, he gave the right to become children of God-' and moreover in verse 11 we are told, rather sadly, that 'His own did not receive Him.' Clearly **receiving** is really vital to God. He does not want us to work in order to earn His favour for, 'it is by grace you have been saved, through faith – and this not from yourselves, it is the gift of God – not by works so that no one can boast.' (Ephesians 2:8,9) God wants none of us boasting when we get to heaven, singing "I did it my way!"

Now we may know this well, but our human propensity to default back to earning, rather than primarily receiving, God's free (to us) gift can easily take us down a side road. If so, thanksgiving for God's generous, giving heart can be a powerful help in getting us back on track, as it will help us to simply receive from our Lord all that we need, both for salvation and for our daily lives. (2 Peter 1:3,4). After all when He was asked "What must we do to do the works that God requires?" Jesus' reply was "The work of God is this: to believe in the one He has sent." (John 6:29).

One of our motto's here in our missional community is – "Receive, Enjoy, Grow, Give". I believe that it is so very important that "Receive" comes first. And of course thanksgiving orientates me towards **receiving** all the grace and gifts that I need daily. It moves me away not just from trying to earn or deserve God's favour, but also from the condemnation the accuser of the brethren will heap on me when, as is inevitable, I fail. I would like to suggest that a default mindset and lifestyle governed by thanksgiving for all God's gifts, goodness and love, from our salvation onwards, will help us to live a life of receiving His grace, love and gifts daily. It will set us up for a life of faith as we believe in 'the one God has sent' – Jesus – and it will act as a very big antidote to our human tendency to slip back into the works that make us feel proud, (Ephesians 2:9), or with which we try to earn God's favour.

'Receiving with thanksgiving' applies of course not just to our initial salvation, but also as we seek to reckon on the fact that I have died with Christ and am now risen with Him; that I am a new creation being changed from one degree of glory to another by the Spirit of God. (Romans 6:1-11, 2 Corinthians 3:18 and 5:17). Thanksgiving leads me into a much better, more biblical, and perhaps less religious life; away from that life of trying to improve the old me by self effort – the old me who died with Christ. There is much thankful receiving and reckoning to be done in this regard every day!

So when fresh challenges come and there is the pressure to work harder to be a good Christian, how much better to hit it with thanksgiving, on the basis that this is another opportunity to look for God's promises of provision, care, protection etc, to be given and received by me. There's nothing wrong with 'Help! Help!' prayers, but I think James nails it in this way: 'If any of you lacks wisdom, he should ask God, who gives generously to all without finding fault, and it will be given to him.' (James 1:5). How much better than a 'Help! Help!' prayer is one that is confident in a God who loves to give generously and doesn't tell us off for needing help. This will probably be a prayer that starts with thanksgiving; a prayer that then positions me to **receive**, because I know that the Lord always gives generously in response to my need.

Activation . . .

Next time there is a challenge (and there will be one soon I'm guessing) give thanks that you have another chance to see how much He loves you, and an opportunity to receive the provision that you need and that He loves to give. Give thanks that you will have another testimony of how good the Lord has been to you, whether it was a big or small problem, and revel in the contrast to when you tried to work things out and solve problems in your own strength.

DAY 328 | Thanksgiving and Asking with Confidence for Material Things

Yesterday we were appreciating the fact that, when it comes to things that will help us to live Godly lives, we can ask God with confidence for His help, because of course the Father will give us anything that helps us to grow into the likeness of his Son; but what about other things? What about asking Him for healing, or for money, for a job, or a car. What about asking Him for a life partner or a child? What about praying for things for others? How can we ask with confidence in these situations, where there can be some uncertainty in our minds about what the Lord's will is, and therefore doubt in our heart as we ask.

I think the key here may be found in Psalm 37:3,4, 'Trust in the Lord and do good; ... Delight yourself in the Lord and he will give you the desires of your heart.' As we take a walk through these verses from Psalm 37, we will see how yet again 'thanksgiving' brings us into a place of confidence and 'faith' as we pray because the psalmist leads us through 'trusting in the Lord', 'doing good', and then 'delighting in the Lord', before we get to, 'and he will give you the desires of your heart'.

'Trust in the Lord and do good'. Well as we have now said, many times this year, one of the best way to build trust in the Lord is by remembering and thanking Him for His past mercies and goodness. As we feed our hearts on all the things that the Lord has done for us, and all His promises, our trust in Him just grows and grows. We can even write our own reciprocal psalm like Psalm 136. We can recount His goodness in times past to ourselves and to one another, with the chorus, 'Give thanks to the Lord for He is good, His love endures forever'. In this way we can increase our trust levels astronomically, and this will also help us to 'do good', because as we remember all the ways in which **we** have been blessed, then it's highly likely that we will want to do the right things, make the right choices, and be a blessing **to others**.

Next in Psalm 37 we read, 'Delight yourself in the Lord' or, in The Passion Translation, 'Make God the utmost delight and pleasure of your life'. Well that too is surely going to involve thanksgiving! When we delight in something it's a bit like 'savouring' our food. We take time to enjoy the sight, the smell and the flavours. You can't rush something if you are 'savouring' it. In the same way 'thanksgiving' slows us down enough to 'savour' God's goodness. Taking time to ruminate over His character, and all the good things He has done for us. Taking time to enjoy His word, His promises and to think about all the things that He has brought into our lives, happens at a much greater depth, if we are doing so with a heart of gratitude. So often the more grateful we are for something or someone, the more beautiful and delightful they become to us; it's a glorious circle.

Then we reach the part where it says, 'and He will give you the desires of your heart.' So how do I know that these desires are OK and in line with His will? That is to say, how can I be sure that He will be happy to give me these things that I desire? Well I believe that as we approach the Lord through this journey of thanksgiving described above, there will also have been a process going on **within** us – very much like the tuning up of a violin. As we thank Him that He is trustworthy and good, and as we savour and take delight in our relationship with Him, our hearts and spirits will gradually be tuned to His 'pitch'. Our spirits will begin to resonate with His. His desires will start to set our desires in the right direction. We will be singing the same song – His song for us! His song that is full of His desires for us; desires that are saturated with His own loving kindness.

Activation . . .

Today before you pray for yourself, or for others, or for any situation you want to bring before Him, give thanks and worship, [pray in tongues too if you have this gift] and let the Holy Spirit fill your heart and mind with God's heart for this moment. You can then pray knowing that the desires of your heart will be coming ever more closely synchronised with His. You will be drawing close to Him and therefore you will be discerning more clearly His will for you at this time and in this situation. Let thanksgiving also 'tune' your heart to His as you pray for others who are on your heart at this time.

DAY 329 | Thanksgiving and the Removal of Rubbish

We have been looking at thanking God for 'giving' us His only Son so that we might have life, and also that we can *ask* Him with confidence for all that we need in order to fully live that new life, to 'live it to the full,' (John 10:10). This is what Jesus Himself would like us to do, so today I was thinking that in addition to *asking* with confidence for the good things that we need, we also need to *ask* Him to take things away. Jesus died, yes indeed, to give me new life, and that also means that He died to take away all my bad stuff.

As I describe on day 356 I once heard a Christmas sermon in which we were encouraged to 'give' Jesus what He came for; the things that we normally hide, the things that spoil our lives, like our sin, our anger, our doubts, unbelief, and our fears. Jesus has bought, with a price, all the things that I need to be set free from, my bad stuff: Because of the cross, it's now legally His. Now that for me is a very liberating thought. I, like many other people, have been brought up 'not to be a nuisance', not to 'trouble other people'. It can lead to a kind of independence that can rob others of their opportunity to connect, to be kind, to care, or to be useful.

Now clearly there is a balance in everything, nobody wants a neighbor who is constantly asking for the proverbial 'cup of sugar', but at the same time it is sad when someone in need shuts the door on any help that we might be offering, especially when that help would be given out of love and not duty, and would bring the giver joy, and not a headache. In the same way our independence when we work hard trying to free ourselves of sin etc, makes God very sad.

The thought that Jesus has already paid the price to take away my 'rubbish' and now lives, one hundred per cent thrilled to pour into me – His well loved child – all that I need of His life, His love, His favour and grace is, as I said, a very liberating thought to one who doesn't want to be 'a nuisance'. It frees me to *ask* Him to remove my rubbish, and to *ask* with confidence. The Holy Spirit working within me, just loves to deal with my 'old man' habits and weaknesses, thereby leaving me free to 'live' from the new me.

Now when I was young, at Christmas time, households were always expected to give their trades people a Christmas Box. The dustmen were included.

It was a way of saying 'Thank you' for a job well done; for the removal of rubbish throughout the year. God will remove our rubbish all year long if we *ask* Him to, and we don't need to wait for Christmas to give Him our thanks. Saying "thank you", is however, an important part of the process. Thanking God every time I give Him some more of my rubbish, releases my faith that the job has been done and it confirms my freedom from that particular sin or habit. Thanksgiving that, because of the cross, my 'old stuff' has been taken away also releases another 'thank you' that enables me to *receive* the blessing that the Lord gives me to replace the 'rubbish'.

In recent years we have learnt, through the ministry of 'Nothing Hidden Ministries'[1], a simple, memorable prayer journey that enables us to ask the Lord to take away our rubbish. It involves:-

i. taking the negative lies, thoughts and feelings that are not part of my new life in Christ and bringing or 'nailing' them to the cross. (Knowing that they have to die there with Jesus). This can include **sinful feelings** like jealousy, anger, doubt, fear, or **unhelpful thoughts** like 'I'm no good', 'God doesn't care', etc.

ii. I then repent of partnering with these thoughts and feelings and I break all the agreement I have made with these lies, negative beliefs and feelings.

iii. I can then ask God to take them all away, (He can't take away what I am still agreeing with, or holding on to hence step ii).

iv. Finally I ask the Holy Spirit to show me what good things He is going to give me to replace the rubbish. (Remembering that He is the Spirit of Truth).

Activation . . .

This has been a powerful tool in our lives and the lives of many others. Praying through this process with a friend can bring even more significant change. Try it! It is an amazing way to grow in faith and confidence, that the old has gone and the new has come. Thanksgiving is, as ever, a powerful way of increasing our faith and confidence for 'asking', for 'letting go' of the rubbish, and 'receiving' the new.

DAY 330 | Thanksgiving and Leadership

When I began this year of writing a daily thanksgiving blog, even though I had frequently advocated a thankful lifestyle, I had no idea how absolutely fundamental and essential thanksgiving was in our relationship with the Lord. It's strange how, once the Lord has brought something to our attention, we 'see' it in places where previously it passed us by. So now, three quarters of the way through the year, I am struck by the number of times that Paul encouraged 'thanksgiving', either by example or by exhortation, and how 'Thanksgiving' permeated his leadership.

If you are now saying, "Well that's not relevant for me, I'm not a leader", please think again. If you 'know' the Lord then you are a leader. This is because we can all lead each other in different aspects of life where we have experience, and we can all lead those 'younger' than us in the faith. Even the newest Christian can now be a leader in leading others to the wonderful Saviour to whom they have now given their life. So let's have a look at Paul's leadership 'ethos'.

He starts his letter with, **'We always thank God,** the Father of our Lord Jesus Christ, when we pray for you, because we have heard of your faith in Christ Jesus and the love you have for all the saints . . .' (Colossians 1:3). Now that is a good habit to develop; to always start your prayers for others with thanksgiving for them and their faith. This is also a good way to start a conversation with someone, by letting them know that you thank God for them. It will open their heart to you and any message that you bring.

After bringing some warnings about false teachers Paul then writes, 'So then, just as you received Christ Jesus as Lord, continue to live in Him, rooted and built up in Him, strengthened in the faith as you were taught, and **overflowing with thankfulness.**' (Colossians 2:6). This is a great example for us because when we are seeking to encourage someone in the faith it is not just about helping them to get their doctrine right, it's about making sure that their hearts are connecting with the Lord by 'overflowing with thankfulness'. Something we have been endeavouring to do ourselves throughout this year.

In the next chapter, Paul addresses them on their attitudes towards each other. In one of the most beautiful passages ever written on how to love each other he writes, 'Therefore as God's chosen people, holy and dearly loved, clothe yourselves with compassion, kindness, humility, gentleness and patience. Bear with each other and forgive whatever grievances you may have against one another. Forgive as the Lord forgave you. And over all these virtues put on love which binds them all together in perfect unity. Let the peace of Christ rule in your hearts, since as members of one body you were called to peace. **And be thankful.**' (Colossians 3:12-15).

He then continues, 'Let the word of Christ dwell in you richly as you teach and admonish one another with all wisdom, and as you sing psalms, hymns and spiritual songs **with gratitude in your hearts to God**. And whatever you do, whether in word or deed, do it all in the name of the Lord Jesus, **giving thanks to God the Father through Him.**' (Colossians 3:16,17). Clearly thanksgiving for each other is like the oil that flows between us, bringing ease and peace between all the members of the body.

In his final greeting Paul exhorts them, 'Devote yourselves to prayer, **being watchful and thankful.**' (Colossians 4:2). And there it is again, an encouragement to stay thankful, even while praying for others with their difficulties and challenges. It is worth reminding ourselves too, that Paul wrote all this encouragement to be thankful not from a comfortable home, but from prison, far from home, and unsure of his future.

Activation ...

In these days of 'Influencers' Paul is indeed someone whose example it is well worth following. Let him be your influencer as you copy his leadership style. Make sure you 'give thanks' for those for whom you are praying; and, when you have the opportunity, encourage them to have a heart of thankfulness themselves. Make sure that you are giving thanks for those you are in relationship with in the body of Christ, and for those you are teaching or leading. Thanksgiving will sweeten all those relationships. Finally make sure that you give thanks even as you are 'watchful' in defending the faith from error and false teaching. It will help to keep those important conversations sharp, but humble and gentle.

DAY 331 | Could I astonish Jesus?

Reading again the story in Matthew 8: 5-13 of Jesus' encounter with the Centurion, my attention was drawn to Jesus' response. You may remember that the Centurion came to Jesus and told Him that his servant was paralysed and in great pain and so Jesus said to him, "I will go and heal him". The Centurion said "Lord I do not deserve to have you come under my roof. But just say the word and my servant will be healed." He tells Jesus that he fully understands how authority works and, by implication, how it will work with Jesus, and so "When Jesus heard this He was **astonished . . .**" And Jesus makes it clear that He was astonished by the man's great faith.

What a great thing it would be to be able to astonish Jesus! To astonish the Son of God! And notice, Jesus wasn't astonished by profound wisdom, deep theology, immense cleverness, amazing wit, or super social skills – the things that may astonish us. If we feel that we lack these things it may make us discount ourselves. "Oh I could never astonish Jesus." We say, "I am not clever enough, I don't understand the bible enough." etc. etc. The Centurion, was a non Jew, who felt totally unworthy for Jesus to visit his house, and yet Jesus was astonished **when He saw his faith**.

It was his straightforward, child-like faith that astonished Jesus. He said, in effect, "**Just** say the word right here Jesus, no need to come to my house and assess the situation." So Jesus responded, clearly He and His Father, really love child-like faith. And then what about the haemorrhaging woman in Matthew 9:21? She had similar child likeness. "If I **only** touch His cloak, I will be healed." "**Only!**" No need for a conversation, an explanation, a justification, or a list of why I deserve it. Simple, straightforward, but great, faith.

How about someone else who excited, perhaps even astonished Jesus with her "great faith"? The Canaanite woman in Matthew 15:21-28. She cried out to Jesus for her cruelly demon possessed daughter. Jesus said nothing. The disciples wanted him to send her away, but she didn't give up. Jesus then seemed to close the door saying, "I was sent only to the lost sheep of the house of Israel." She wasn't an Israelite – so she wasn't included. She still didn't give up and Jesus still seems to keep the door shut. "It is not right to take the children's bread and toss it to their dogs." She doesn't take offence. She isn't insulted, but instead she lets this interaction with Jesus draw out a beautiful response.

She shares a wonderful, wonderful moment of revelation saying, in effect, "I may be unworthy, but I believe that you and your Father are so generous, and there is so much love and power in your heart Lord, that even the 'left overs' of your love and power falling from the children's table will heal my daughter." Wow. I think Jesus was excited. She had got it, how big, generous, spilling over, bursting out of the banks, the 'not proper' love of God, is. What a stark comparison to the Pharisees; the clever men, with their narrow, contained view of God and of His ways and character.

It is interesting that both the centurion and the Canaanite woman felt unworthy, but this didn't diminish their faith. Instead it produced genuine humility, and simple but strong faith in a hugely generous God. I think there is something here on which we need the Holy Spirit to give us some child-like revelation. **Great faith is not about how much faith we have but about the greatness of the one in whom we have faith.** This is why Jesus could talk about faith as a grain of mustard seed having great power. A mustard seed is tiny but it's packed with the right DNA to produce a very large fruitful plant. If my faith is in who Jesus is, as opposed to how big I feel that my faith is, it will be packed with the right 'faith' DNA. Giving thanks is therefore one of the best ways in which to build our faith. It will make it more likely for us to approach Jesus like the centurion, or those two ladies, confident of what He can do, even when we feel unworthy.

Activation ...

Today be like the Canaanite woman. Don't be put off by the lack of (apparent) initial response, but rather astonish Jesus by saying, 'I know that You are generous beyond measure in Your love, power and care for me and those I love, and that You will come through for me even if I feel unworthy. Let the simple act of thanksgiving get your focus away from your 'faith level' and onto the Lord Jesus. Grow in childlike faith so that it may then become 'great faith' and 'astonish' Him.

DAY 332 | Thanksgiving, an 'Elixir of Youth'?

In Psalm 92:12-14 we read, 'The righteous will flourish like a palm tree, they will grow like a cedar of Lebanon; planted in the house of the Lord, they will flourish in the **court**s of our God. They will still bear fruit in old age, they will stay fresh and green, proclaiming, "Lord is upright; he is my Rock, and there is no wickedness in him.' This suggested to me that in order to flourish and bear lots of fruit, and in order to thrive and stay 'fresh' even in old age we need to be found often in the **courts** of our God. In fact we need to be actually 'planted in the house of the Lord.'

Since the bible is often the best commentary on itself we can turn to other psalms as we ponder what this actually means and explore what the Psalms tell us about the '**courts of our God**'? Well, as we noted on Day 1 of our journey, we can enter those courts with thanksgiving, (Psalm 100:4). And the psalmist who wrote Psalm 84 yearns for those courts telling God that 'those who dwell in your house; they are ever praising you'. (verses 1-4). David in Psalm 65:4 tells us that the ones chosen to be brought near to live in those courts, 'are filled with the good things' of God's house.

It is no wonder then that David in Psalm 27:4-6 says that there is one thing that He has asked of the Lord, 'that I may dwell in the house of the Lord all the days of my life,' because there he beholds 'the delightful loveliness of the Lord...' (AMP) This all sounds like there is a great deal of worship and communion there and also safety and protection. So he offers up sacrifices with shouts of joy, as he sings and makes music to the Lord.

In Psalm 96:8,9 we are further encouraged to, 'Ascribe to the Lord the glory due his name; bring an offering and **come into his courts**. Worship the Lord in the splendour of his holiness.' Or consider Psalm 135:2,3, 'You who stand in the house of the Lord, **in the courts** of the house of our God.' (where we now know we flourish and stay fruitful in old age) 'Praise the Lord, for the Lord is good; sing praise to his name, for it is lovely.' (NASB). I think we can conclude that thanksgiving, praise and worship clearly permeate everything that is going on in the courts of the house of the Lord. And so we can link the promise of Psalm 92, that if I am planted in the courts of the house of the Lord I will flourish and still be fruitful in my old age, as I praise and worship.

A couple of thoughts: 'planted' suggests that I am not in and out. The limited gardener in me knows that if trees keep being moved about they don't do so well, the roots need to stay put. Developing the attitude of gratitude, leading to a daily lifestyle of thanksgiving, reflected in frequent, daily, steady, thanksgiving, praise and worship will cause my roots to settle, and I will be 'planted' and therefore flourishing rather than being stunted. I will also not be easily moved from that place.

Secondly this is not a self-centred flourishing in old age:- retired, slippers on, do what pleases me. Yes, it is a retirement from the warfare of work, and the sweat involved in that (See Numbers 8:24-26), but that is not the end of fruitfulness. It is rather moving to a more restful lifestyle in which to flourish, because it is clear in Psalm 92:14 that they will still yield fruit and will still be green, that is shining and beautiful, and full of sap; still flowing in ministry, (Numbers 8:26).

This flourishing and fruitfulness will bring glory to Jesus, and life, healing and the good news of salvation to many. This also resonates with Jesus' words about letting our light shine. Shining both because of His life in us and because of the things that we do. Yet again our friend Caleb seems a great biblical example. He was definitely still flourishing, fruitful and full of sap at age 85. (Joshua 14:10-12)

Activation . . .

So let us take on board how interwoven gratitude, thanksgiving, praise and worship are with being planted in the courts of the house of the Lord, and how the Holy Spirit has indicated that being planted and settled there is where we flourish and are fruitful even at a time of life when we can't run as fast, walk as far, or pack quite as much into every twenty four hours. What a thrilling promise and encouragement for us to move towards an even greater and more frequent flow of thanksgiving, praise and worship.

DAY 333 | Thanksgiving a Sign of My Agreement with God

In 2 Corinthians chapter 1, Paul is explaining his change of plan to his friends in the church at Corinth. It seems likely that they were disappointed, perhaps even critical of his change of plan. It is possible therefore that Paul felt that he was appearing to be vacillating and therefore unreliable, because in verse 17 he asks, '... do I make my plans in a worldly manner so that in the same breath I say, "Yes, yes" and "No, no"?

It was in this context that Paul makes the wonderful statement that 'the Son of God, Jesus Christ . . . was not "Yes" and "No" but in him it has always been "Yes". For no matter how many promises God has made, they are "Yes" in Christ. And so through Him the "Amen" is spoken by us to the glory of God.' (2 Corinthians 1:19,20). Paul was explaining that not only was he not a vacillator, but that God Himself is most definitely not, and that if God has made a promise it will find it's "Yes", it's fulfillment in Jesus. Remember that Jesus said to Philip, "Anyone who has seen me has seen the Father." (John 14:9). Jesus and His Father are completely one, and whatever promise Father God speaks, Jesus will fulfill and complete it.

Paul is telling us that Jesus is always totally in unison with the Father when it comes to God's will and His promises, so I think we can say, with certainty, that it is God's desire that we, being confident that Jesus never lies, will always be saying "Amen" as a sign that we believe in the fulfillment of God's promises through Jesus. What then does it mean to say "Amen"? Well we could use the phrase "So be it". It is just like saying, "I believe Father, that the promise you made is true and will work for me because of Jesus."

"So be it" is a very positive affirmation but I personally think that, in our day and age, it can have a slightly down beat fatalistic edge to it. We can imagine someone who has just received some bad news saying, "So be it" in an attempt to agree with their fate. For this reason I prefer the Message paraphrase for "Amen", and that is written as a resounding, "Oh Yes!"

If we look for example at the moment in heaven when every creature in heaven and earth join in the worship of the Lamb, (Revelation 5:13,14), the four living creatures shout "Oh Yes!" and 'The elders fall to their knees and worship.' Or read the last words in the Bible. Jesus says "I am coming soon", and the reply is, "Oh Yes, Come Master Jesus!" (Revelation 22:20,21, The Message). For me, the "Oh Yes" conveys a very strong shout of true faith.

When God says that He will never leave us, that He has and will forgive all my sins, that He will meet all my needs, and so much more, saying "Amen", "So be it", or "Oh Yes", by way of agreeing with God, is very close to saying "Thank you". "Thank you that you will never leave me." "Thank you that you forgive all my sins." "Thank you that you will supply all my needs according to His glorious riches in Christ Jesus." Speaking out our thanksgiving is often the action needed to activate our faith, and make it real. I also think that thanksgiving is one of the 'works' that demonstrates how real our faith is. (See James 2:14-26). Thanksgiving is a very practical way of saying "Amen" and "Oh Yes" to God's promises that are, have been, and will be fulfilled to us in Jesus.

Activation . . .

The prophet Amos asks, 'do two men walk together unless they have agreed to do so?' (Amos 3:3), and so we learn that, walking with the Lord involves agreement with Him. Thanksgiving is a great way of coming into agreement more fully with the Lord and His promises, and thus walking in closer, more intimate and more sweetly satisfying friendship with Him on a daily basis.

Today express your faith and agreement with God by saying your "Amen" or your "Oh Yes" to God through your thanksgiving. This brings such glory to God, and will thrill his heart for He has found a person who wants to walk in close agreement with Him.

DAY 334 | Thanksgiving, Caves and Risk

I was recently in a conversation with a friend, who was feeling at a low place in life and in her faith, and I made a suggestion that I thought would help her to move forward. Her reply was, "That means taking a risk." To which I said, "Yes it does." It felt like she was in a cave, a place she had retreated to for 'emotional safety', and that she was afraid to come out. It reminded me of Elijah, sat in his cave in despair and despondency, and God's question to him, "What are you doing here Elijah?" (1 Kings 19:9).

Now Elijah was a man who, in an extraordinary display of boldness and faith, had called down fire from heaven to defeat the prophets of Baal. (1 Kings 18:20-40). He had won this amazing victory by taking a huge risk that God would be with him; would honour his words, and back him up with power. He demonstrated what I had heard years ago, in a sermon on faith, that FAITH can also be spelt RISK!!

So Elijah, probably one of the most powerful of the prophets and a big risk taker, was having his life threatened by Jezebel. She wanted revenge for the killing of her prophets, so he ran away and found a cave. In a very similar way we can find ourselves at one moment full of faith and happy to take a faith-risk and then, even within the same day, withdrawing into ourselves; hiding from people, and not feeling like moving very far from the spot.

This 'cave mentality', as I like to call it, can also follow some personal hurt, rejection, or disappointment. Often in life it can seem easier to take a risk in what can look like an openly public work of faith, than to risk coming out of our cave when we have been hurt or rejected. How often do we say to God when something has gone wrong, "I'm not doing that again", or "I'm not going there again". Effectively we are saying to God," I'm not coming out! It's not safe." And He, I think, would say to us, as He did to Elijah, "What are you doing here ... (put in your name)?"

What happened next for Elijah is surely one of the most beautiful moments in the Old Testament. The Lord listens to Elijah's take on his situation, then says to him, "Go and stand on the mountain in the presence of the Lord, for the Lord is about to pass by." It's the last thing he wants to do, to expose himself again, so Elijah, it would appear, stays put. Then the really powerful tornado like wind, the rock shattering earthquake and the fire all come and go, after which Elijah hears 'a gentle whisper', something like a breath, and only then does he manage to get to the mouth of the cave, and there he meets with God.

God asks him the same question, "What are you doing here Elijah?", so he tells God his problem all over again. Then he gets his instructions from the Lord as to what to do, and who to link up with. It is also revealed to him that far from being the only one left (as he thought) there are 7,000 who have not gone over to Baal's side. Elijah needed to come out of His cave to hear all of that and to get the instructions he needed to get on with his life, and God knew that it was His gentle whisper, not the display of power, that would draw him out. (1Kings 19:9-18).

It just seems to me that when faced with a 'cave' moment (day, week, year?) I will stay in my cave as long as I keep ruminating on the problems I have had, or that I might face if I come out. I need to do something more than tell God the problem, I need to position myself to see His power and His might, (wind, fire and earthquake) and I need to step out of my cave in order to hear and see His gentleness, kindness, care and future plans for me. I think David understood this. In his wonderful Psalm written when the Lord delivered him from King Saul, he sings to the Lord 'Your gentleness makes me great'. (2 Samuel 22:36, Psalm 18:35, NASB).

Activation ...

It is always the enemy who wants to keep you in the cave with his lies and fear. So if you ever find yourself in a cave, instead of ruminating on the hurt, or the problems ahead try, with thanksgiving, to remember God's power and glory. Let thanksgiving focus your heart on Jesus, and His love for you. Let thanksgiving bring you close to Him so that you can hear His whisper and run into His arms of love. Then what previously seemed like an impossible risk may start to feel more like a manageable adventure. Build your faith with thanksgiving until you have the courage to step out of your cave into the gentle arms of the Lord. Let Him lead you forward as you remember that His plans are to 'prosper you and not to harm you,' (Jeremiah 29:11)

DAY 335 | Thanksgiving, and 'Looking Back'

One of the difficulties of life is the fact that it is not a rehearsal. As we go through life we are learning on the job. We are therefore doing many things for the first time. We are potentially learning and growing all the time but we make many mistakes as we gain experience and wisdom. It is then easy to look back and say to ourselves, "**if only** I had known that then", or "**If only** I could have that time again with what I know now."

Our growing life experience and wisdom can then turn from '**if only**' into regret, and regret is a very unhelpful emotion. It is different to repentance. Repentance can help us to leave the past behind, and to learn from it. The wrong kind of regret can weigh us down. It keeps us looking at past mistakes, failures, and inadequacies, which then make it harder to look forward with hope, faith and expectancy.

While God, many times, asks His people not to 'forget' His goodness, His kindness, and His acts on their behalf, He Himself promises to remove our transgressions from us and remember our sins no more. (See Psalm 103:2 & 12 and Isaiah 43:25). He doesn't dwell on our past mistakes and failures, and nor should we. Dwelling on the past in a negative way with regret is not only unhelpful but it does not honour Jesus, who died that we might be free to live for Him, unfettered by our past.

Then there is the looking back with 'longing' for past things. God knows that 'looking back' in the wrong way doesn't work for us either, and so He tells His people not to 'look back' on several occasions. When His people have disobeyed Him, when they have 'looked back', they have lost faith and have got themselves into trouble. The Israelites for example, just a couple of months after they had come out of Egypt, were looking back with nostalgia and it distorted their vision.

They then said "If only we had died by the Lord's hand in Egypt! There we sat around pots of meat and ate all the food we wanted, but you have brought us out to starve this entire assembly to death." (Exodus 16:3). They also remembered the fish, the cucumbers, melons, leeks, onions and garlic that they had previously had, and they began to grumble and complain.

(Numbers 11:5). Unbelievable!! They had been badly treated slaves. No memory here then of making bricks without enough straw? How sad that the mighty deliverance they had seen from Egypt and as they crossed the Red Sea, was lost to them as they dwelt on the wrong memories.

And why was Lot's wife told not to look back? Would it provoke longing, nostalgia, regrets? Whatever it was, it wasn't helpful. Instead of being thankful for the incredible deliverance they had experienced as they ran into their future with the Lord she, it would appear, still had her heart in Sodom. Looking back certainly didn't work for her. (Genesis 19:17 & 26). God did not want them to be drawn back into their past.

We can also look back unhealthily to past triumphs. We can be regretful that a time of success, or a great season in life, seems to be passing by all too quickly with time and age. The regret, 'if only that had gone on longer', can hinder us from healthy grieving and 'moving on'. If we find ourselves dwelling nostalgically on the past we need to check out whether our heart is more in the past than in our future with the Lord. We need to be like Paul who declared, 'Forgetting what is behind and straining towards what is ahead, I press on toward the goal to win the prize for which God has called me heavenward in Christ Jesus.' (Philippians 3:13,14).

God doesn't want us living in the past with too much regret, or with too much nostalgia So if we are going to look back, it needs to be fully 'laced' with 'thanksgiving'. Thanksgiving that past mistakes and sins have been 'covered'; thanksgiving for past deliverances and blessing; thanksgiving for past fruitfulness, and definitely thanksgiving for the future because, in Christ, the mantra 'The best is yet to come' makes sense. We truly are the only people on earth who can fully embrace that saying, because not only are we being transformed day by day to be more and more like Jesus we are also looking forward to a blissful eternity with Father, Son and Holy Spirit.

Activation . . .

Because the Lord is in your future, give thanks today for the past and lessons learnt. Give thanks for the good times enjoyed and like David declare with confidence, **'Surely (definitely) goodness and loving kindness will follow me all the days of my life, and I will dwell in the house of the Lord forever.'** (Psalm 23:6,NASB).

DAY 336 | Thanksgiving and Praying in Faith

Sometimes, even when we have understood that praying is not about bending God's will to fit ours, we can still find it hard to know what exactly Jesus meant when He said, "... the Father will give you whatever you ask in my name." (John 15:16). How do I know that that for which I am asking, fits with what Jesus would be asking for? I think it comes down to seeing the situation, or the person for whom I am praying, through His eyes.

So apart from rising above the challenges that life throws up and finding God's peace in the 'storms' of life, waiting on the Lord, or 'entwining our heart' with His, (Isaiah 40:31), brings another blessing. As we wait on Him and 'rise up on eagles wings' we begin to see things more clearly from God's perspective. This then radically alters our prayer life, shifting us from trying to persuade the Lord to work according to our ideas of what would be good, towards sensing what is on His heart. Waiting on the Lord can help to bring us into agreement with His will, and then we can pray 'in faith.'

Matthew in his gospel recounts a mysterious conversation that Jesus had with Peter. Jesus says to him, "I will give you the keys of the Kingdom of heaven; and whatever you bind on earth shall have been bound in heaven, and whatever you loose on earth shall have been loosed in heaven." Jesus uses that phrase again at a later point, this time speaking to all the disciples, "Truly I say to you, whatever you bind on earth shall have been bound in heaven; and whatever you loose on earth shall have been loosed in heaven. Again I say to you, that if two of you agree on earth about anything that they may ask for, it shall be done for them by my Father who is in heaven. For where two or three have gathered together in my name, I am there in their midst." (Matthew 16:19, and 18:18-20, NASB).

Jesus is here indicating that there can be complete harmony between those disciples and each other, and between the disciples and heaven; that they could 'know' and respond to God's will and what was unfolding in heaven. Effective prayer then, involves a lot of agreement. Agreement among God's people, and agreement between God's people and God in heaven. So how can we individually, or as a group together, say 'your will be done on earth as it is in heaven' not as a fatalistic statement because we don't really know what is going on, but as a statement of faith? (Matthew 6:10).

I believe we can increasingly pray 'your will be done on earth as it is in heaven,' with faith in our hearts as we 'wait upon the Lord'. Rising up as if on eagles wings, we can take our place, in the spirit, in the heavenly realms, and so pray in harmony with heaven. For me this is why no time of prayer can 'work' without us spending some time 'waiting' on the Lord. Whether we are on our own or with others. As we turn our hearts to Him with thanksgiving and worship, we catch the thermals of His love and soar with Him into that heavenly realm.

As we worship we will grow in our ability to hear His Spirit and catch His heart. Then as we pray we won't be persuading God to fulfill our agenda, but we will increasingly sense the mind of God, hearing the conversations in heaven and be able, by the power of the indwelling Spirit, to agree with our God. As we soar with Him, above the situations that we are carrying in prayer, we will increasingly 'see' what needs to be bound or loosed, and increasingly 'hear' what heaven has already done. Then in agreement with each other and with the Lord we can, with faith, pray our prayers and say, 'Your will be done on earth as it is in heaven.'

As we have said previously, thanksgiving is such an important key to 'waiting on the Lord'. It keeps our focus off of the 'problem' and raises our sights to heaven where God's will is always done. It also helps us to gain the revelation that we need to have in prayer, because whatever battles are being played out on the earth, Jesus has already won in heaven. Thanksgiving feeds our faith in the Lord, His purposes, His plans, His goodness, His love and His power. We can then pray 'with faith', raising our spiritual high 5's of victory, even before things are played out on the earth.

Activation . . .

Next time you pray, on your own or with others, lift your heart to the Lord in grateful praise and worship before you tell Him what you want Him to do for you. Even praying with one other person in this way will increase your ability to discern God's will as you 'soar' together, hear from heaven, gain the 'mind of Christ' and pray 'in agreement'.

DAY 337 | Thanksgiving that Magnifies the Lord

One of the passages of scripture that I knew long before I was a Christian was 'the Magnificat'. We sang it Sunday by Sunday in the church I attended as a young person. It's Mary's song of praise to the Lord, which she spoke out after Elizabeth had prophetically confirmed the Angel's message to her, telling her that she would indeed have a baby and that He would be the long awaited Messiah. (Luke 1:31,32 and 42,43). The song is called the Magnificat because, as the Authorised Version translates it, Mary starts by saying, 'My soul doth **Magnify** the Lord,' (Luke 1:46).

Later, after I had become a Christian and we sang a newer version of her song, I always wondered why we needed to magnify God. I thought magnification was about making something bigger, but surely we can never add to God, or make Him any bigger than He really is, and we certainly wouldn't be able to make Him any bigger just by singing a song written a couple of thousand years ago.

Magnification, however, is not about making anything literally bigger, but it is about enlarging the appearance of something, in order to be able to see it more clearly than we can with the naked eye. David, celebrating his escape from Abimelech, calls on others to '**magnify the Lord**' with him. He wants others to be able to see more clearly how good God has been to him, in order that they might put their trust in Him too. He sings "My soul will make its boast in the Lord; the humble will hear it and rejoice. O **magnify** the Lord with me, and let us exalt His name together.' (Psalm 34:2,3. NASB).

When the Holy Spirit fell on the gentiles in Cornelius' household, Peter and his friends were astonished 'For they heard them speak with tongues, and **magnify** God.' (Acts 10:46, AV). They were, by praising God in tongues and their own languages, speaking out for all to hear how mighty God is. Other translations instead of magnify speak of 'extolling', 'glorifying', or 'exalting' the Lord. Whatever word we use, it is clearly about lifting Him up with our praise so that all can see more clearly what a wonderful God He is.

It is, however, not just God who we can magnify. We can also magnify the work of the enemy, our problems, or someone else's faults and failings. It's not difficult to do. Magnifying something involves putting a lens in front of the thing and focusing on it to the exclusion of other things. Sometimes we can be aware of the fact that the more we focus on a thing the bigger it seems to be in our minds eye.

Sometimes, when I am out for a walk for example, I can find myself focusing, not on the wonderful vista before me, but on the new housing estate that has been built down the hill, which now covers up a smallish field and catches the corner of my eye. It's so easy for things which annoy or trouble us to 'fill our gaze' and preoccupy our minds. They become ever more magnified as we dwell and ruminate on them. In such situations the antidote for me is to intentionally thank the Lord for the 'good' things, and thereby turn my attention away from the irritations to **magnify** the blessings.

Paul tells us in Philippians 4:8, to 'ponder' or 'let our mind dwell on' (NASB) things that are noble, right, pure, lovely, admirable, excellent, and praiseworthy, and gratitude for such things certainly helps to focus our attention on them. Giving thanks for those 'good' things is a wonderful way to **magnify** what is good and right in any situation in life. And, as we speak out with thankfulness about the goodness of God in our lives, we **magnify Him** to those around us. Our testimony can then draw others into God's Kingdom, especially those who are struggling to live life without Him.

Another of David's psalms spells this out very clearly for us. 'I am afflicted and in pain; may your salvation, O God, set me *securely* on high. I will praise the Lord, the name of God with a song and **magnify Him with thanksgiving**. And it will please the Lord better than an ox or a young bull ... The humble have seen it *and* are glad; You who seek God, let your heart revive. For the Lord hears the needy and does not despise His *who are* prisoners.' (Psalm 69:29-33, NASB).

Activation ...

Determine to, '**Magnify the Lord**' and make His name great by your thankfulness. Make His name great in your family, your workplace and your neighbourhood, so that the 'humble (or afflicted) will hear and be glad.' (Psalm 34:2).

DAY 338 | Thanksgiving that releases more blessing

We watched a nature program yesterday which explored an amazing, but unseen, event that takes place in the rainforest. We were shown how an apparently insignificant fungus, which lives on, or sometimes unseen below, the forest floor, is actually the agent that causes the torrential rain to fall. This fungus releases tiny microscopic spores that become airborne. They are so light that they are carried up, on the slightest breeze, into the damp atmosphere where they 'seed' the water vapour. As they combine in this way with the water vapour droplets of rain form. These droplets then fall as the vast quantities of rain that gives the forest its name.

We spoke yesterday of how our thanksgiving can 'magnify the Lord'; how 'thanksgiving' focuses our attention, and that of others, onto the goodness of God so that we see Him and all His kindness, goodness, power and might more clearly. Today as I was thinking about the 'forest floor fungus', I sensed that the Lord would speak to us prophetically through the powerful effect of those tiny fungus spores, and their power to produce torrential rain. He wants us, His people to know that our thanksgiving does more than magnify Him to the world, our thanksgiving rises up to heaven, and becomes a significant part of releasing, into our world, all that God has in His heart.

As we give thanks, we magnify the Lord and focus our attention on His story, not the enemy's, and as our thanks is received in heaven it 'seeds' the vast amount of blessing that is stored up there, both for ourselves and for others. We become the agents which cause the 'rain of heaven', the blessings of God to 'fall' upon the earth. What a mighty lesson from nature this is.

I might feel that my thanksgiving is small, even weak and insignificant, or I may feel that I have very little to give thanks for today, but how good it will be if I can see that all those small, even insignificant moments, of 'giving thanks' are rising up to the Father's heart, and 'seeding' the blessing that He wants to pour out. Then I think I will want to pray like Frances Ridley

Havergal did 150 years ago through her hymn, 'Take my life and let it be consecrated, Lord to thee'.[1] In one of the verses she writes, **'Take my moments and my days let them flow in ceaseless praise.'**

When we see the power of our thanksgiving to 'seed' and bring down the rain from heaven, we will be like Paul when we are praying for others. Remember how he wrote and told the Ephesians, **'I have not stopped giving thanks** for you, remembering you in my prayers.' (Ephesians 1:16). Wouldn't we all like to be prayed for like that – with unceasing thanksgiving. So in our praying let us not just focus on the problems and difficulties in life, or in the life of another, but let us magnify the Lord by thanking Him for what He has already done, or begun to do. Then, as we pray, our thanksgiving will be 'seeding' the further blessings that we are looking for from the Lord, both for ourselves and others.

I believe that the Lord wants us His people to grow into a 24/7 lifestyle of thanksgiving. In heaven thanksgiving is 'ceaseless'. The four living creatures **ceaselessly** honour the Lord saying, 'HOLY, HOLY, HOLY *is* THE LORD GOD, THE LORD ALMIGHTY WHO WAS AND WHO IS AND WHO IS TO COME.' (Revelation 4:8, NASB). So let it be 'on earth as in heaven'. Let us be ceaseless in our thanksgiving, and increasingly keep our hearts filled with gratitude at all times, and in all situations, for His glory, and for the further blessing both of ourselves and others.

Activation . . .

'Let your joy be a continual feast. Make your life a prayer. **And in the midst of everything be always giving thanks, for this is God's perfect plan for you in Christ Jesus.'** (1 Thessalonians 5:16-18.TPT).

Have faith in your heart today that as you give thanks, you are seeding the heavens and the rain of blessing is going to fall.

DAY 339 | Thanksgiving that Touches Heaven and Changes Earth

Yesterday, we looked at the power of our thanksgiving to 'seed' the rain of blessing from heaven, in the same way that the tiny spores from the fungus on the rain forest floor rise up on the breeze and turn water vapour into drops of rain. The power of that picture stays with me, especially since the fungus which releases those tiny spores that seed the rain, actually grows by nourishing itself on rotting matter, dead trees and leaves; things that are defunct in terms of their useful fruit bearing life.

Nature is so wonderful that in all kinds of ways one year's dead cells become the fertiliser, compost and nourishment for the following year's new growth, and so it occurred to me that even in those situations where things seem to have gone wrong and, as it were, 'died'; we can still offer up our thanks for the good things that God will work through those situations.

It never ceases to amaze me that, even when I seem to have 'messed up', (big time, or barely noticeable) if I can turn that situation over to the Lord offering up my mistakes and sin to Him, with thanksgiving, He will come to my rescue and use what would appear to be dead and useless in my life to fertilise fresh growth in the days and weeks ahead. Our God is just so good at forgiving us and then turning even our failures into triumph, if we offer them to Him with our thanks.

As I stay in thankfulness, the Lord can give me the grace to apologise if I need to, or the wisdom to address the circumstances in which I find myself. He will lead me to overcome evil with good, or bless those who I feel are persecuting me. He will provide for me if I have been foolish with my use of resources, and give me strength when I don't deserve it because I have been self willed. As I offer up my thanksgiving He will be releasing from heaven undeserved grace and favour, just because He loves me and He can.

Now it is important to remind ourselves that thanksgiving is not a magic wand, it is not a mantra, or a rain dance, which is used to invoke the god's to send the rain, but it is about relationship. The reason that thanksgiving is so different to all these other 'pseudo religious' practices is that, thanksgiving is not about our efforts to wind up some kind of positivity, it's not about earning God's favour, but it is all about developing a closer relationship with our Heavenly Father.

Being thankful, for His forgiveness, His never failing love, His grace and help in my weaknesses draws me into an ever closer relationship with my Heavenly Father. As I acknowledge who He is and what He has already done, my thanksgiving turns my heart and focus from all my failures and mistakes, and draws me into God's arms of love. Then as we said yesterday, our thanksgiving can, because it 'connects' us more deeply with God's heart of love, become a mystical but significant means of releasing into our world all that God has in His heart.

I am convinced that, in our various challenging situations, thanksgiving for the amazing grace of God is so powerful that it will, like the spores that trigger the rainfall, release further blessing from God into that situation. This will not be because we have earned it, but because He loves to forgive and redeem any situation which we offer up to Him. He loves to respond to the love and faith we are expressing. In this way thanksgiving becomes a powerful way in which we find ourselves 'Touching Heaven and Changing Earth.' And this is because thanksgiving unlike doubt, discouragement and unbelief, is the language of heaven and the key to entering His courts. (Psalm 100:4).

Activation . . .

Next time you feel a failure or that you have messed up in some way, instead of self recrimination, self justification or self effort to put whatever is wrong right, turn with your whole heart to the Lord with thankfulness for who He is and for His incredible ability to forgive and make wrong things right. Let your thankfulness release the spores that will make the rain of heaven fall on your life and the lives of those around you.

Remember . . .

'Let joy your be a continual feast. Make your life a prayer. **And in the midst of everything be always giving thanks, for this is God's perfect plan for you in Christ Jesus.**' (1 Thessalonians 5:16-18. TPT).

DAY 340 | Thanksgiving, Mercy and Humility

Today the word that I think the Lord would have us ruminate on is 'Mercy'. So I looked up the Oxford Dictionary definition and was blown away. It said, Mercy, n. **Compassion shown by one to another who is in his power and has no claim to kindness.** then by way of an added explanation; **that is a ... mercy ..., (a blessing, thing to be thankful for).**

'Mercy' in this day and age is not a fashionable topic of conversation. It is more often linked to the idea of the gangster who will show 'no mercy'. It's about a power imbalance and so pleading for mercy is associated with being weak and beholden to a bully. When it comes to current attitudes to God there is a sense, very often, that somehow He owes us. Far from asking Him for mercy, the people around us can think that He should be answerable to us for the things that go wrong in our lives and in the world. Many people, even if they are aware of sin, don't believe that they need God's forgiveness and if they do they may have a general feeling that it is God's job to forgive, and allow us into heaven. This sense of entitlement, often has a harmful effect on the tender relationship between man and his Creator God.

The prophet Jeremiah, however, got it right. Here was a man who was, at times, indignant for the way God seemed to be allowing him to be treated; after all he was prophesying as God wanted him to. In Lamentations 3:1-18, we hear his complaint and how he feels that God has been persecuting him through his enemies. It's really worth a read, and it concludes, 'So I say "My strength has perished, and *so has* my hope from the Lord." (NASB). But then he remembers something. He calls to mind who God is, and he gains new hope, and this is what he remembers. '*It is of* the Lord's mercies that we are not consumed, because His compassions fail not. *They are* new every morning; great is thy faithfulness. The Lord is my portion, saith my soul; therefore will I hope in Him.' (Lamentation 3:21-24, AV).

Jeremiah gets things back into perspective. We were created and given life, because of God's great love and desire to share His glory with us. Sinful as we are, we are 'not consumed' simply because of His mercy. We stay alive because He gives us breath day by day. We are saved from banishment from His presence because of the blood of His Son which covers all our sin. Sin which, but for His mercy through the cross, we would still be carrying. And if we were still carrying it, that sin would prevent us from coming into His courts and living as His well loved children, saturated daily with His blessing.

God owes us nothing. Rather, in order to receive 'mercy', we need to recognise our need for it and we need to remember who we are and who God is. We need to be like the Psalmist who wrote, 'As a father has compassion on his children, so the Lord has compassion on those that fear him; for he knows how we are formed, he remembers that we are dust.' (Psalm 103:13,14). Remembering that 'we are but dust', is not about groveling to a bully, but humbly positioning ourselves before our creator, to receive His undeserved mercy and grace.

It is interesting that in Jesus time, (no welfare state) people more easily seemed to recognise that they needed the mercy of God. Blind Bartimaeus leads the charge here. "Jesus, Son of David, have mercy on me!" (Mark 10:47). The ten lepers too, "Jesus, Master, have mercy on us!" (Luke 17:13, NASB). Asking for mercy, as opposed to claiming our rights, involves acknowledging our need and being humble. Even the Canaanaite woman, who Jesus tested by refusing her initial request, came humbly but with persistence and called on Jesus for mercy. (Matthew 15:22-28).

After describing His glory as His goodness, God said to Moses, "I will have mercy on whom I will have mercy, and I will have compassion on whom I will have compassion." (Exodus 33:19). Let us remember that releasing mercy to us is God's sole prerogative! And thanksgiving for God's daily mercies will, I believe, help us with that. Thanksgiving will keep us not just grateful, but humble.

Activation . . .

Let your gratitude prevent you from taking anything for granted. Not His mercy and forgiveness, not His provision and His grace, nor the air you breathe, or the food you eat. Give thanks for your health and strength, family and friends, home, and job, in fact the whole of life. It will keep you humbly receiving all the good things that the Lord – **in His mercy and grace** – loves to pour out on you daily.

DAY 341 | Thanksgiving and Our Imagination

One of the amazing gifts that God has given mankind is the ability to imagine, to dream, to picture things that are not immediately present. We can recall things in our minds eye from the past and even imagine future possibilities. Because this is the sort of gift that can get us into trouble, we Christians can be wary of using it. Eve for example was tempted, not just by a piece of fruit, (she had access to many delicious fruits) but by the thought that, "your eyes will be opened, and you will be like God, knowing good and evil." (Genesis 3:5). She could imagine that possibility and concluded that God was withholding something good from them, and so she sinned.

Imagination is in itself neither good nor evil, and it is one of the ways in which God has poured into mankind His own creativity. It is behind man's ability to invent both good, even life saving things, as well as the harmful ones. Imagination can also greatly help us in our relationship with God. Both Jesus and the Holy Spirit use metaphor and pictures to help us to understand spiritual principles. We can imagine, for example the shepherd leaving the ninety nine and going off to look for the one. We can imagine the joy of the woman when she found her lost coin (her future security) and the celebration she had with her friends, and so we get a glimpse of how the angels rejoice over one sinner who repents. (Luke 15:3-10).

Good, Holy Spirit led, imagination can aid us in our praying and cause our faith to grow. Conversely, the enemy can use our imagination to unsettle us, intimidate us, causing us to feel fear and anxiety. Worry, after all, is just imagining what might be bad, before it has happened, and without God's grace in the moment. Worry is actually negative imagination leading to negative faith which is 'unbelief'. No wonder then that Jesus told His followers several times "Take no anxious thought" or "Do not worry about your life...food...clothes..." Why did He say that they shouldn't worry? – "because your heavenly Father knows that you need them". (Matthew 6:32). Worry in this case would be about imagining running out of the basic requirements for life, without factoring a very loving Heavenly Father.

In Isaiah 26:3 we have that wonderful promise, 'You will keep in perfect peace him whose mind is steadfast, because he trusts in you.' The only problem is that, when we are feeling anxious, keeping our mind steadfastly on the Lord is hard. Our thoughts can run riot, not wanting to stay focused on the Lord. So it is good to know that the root of that word 'mind', in this context, is in fact the same as 'the imagination'. The Passion Translation puts it like this, 'Perfect, absolute peace surrounds those whose imaginations are consumed with You. They confidently trust in You.' The AV translates this as a mind 'stayed on God'. Simply put, peace comes to us when we can keep our imagination steady and fixed, or 'stayed', on God.

Nature hates a vacuum and so does our mind. If we just try to block out the anxious thoughts, we do not find peace. We need instead to replace the worrying imaginations with good and peaceful thoughts, and so we come again to the gift that is thanksgiving. Through thanksgiving we can anchor our thoughts; 'stay our minds', on all the wonderful things God has done for us, what He promises us, and who He want to be for us. We can draw from our own past testimony and the testimonies of other people. Then as we keep our mind steadfastly on Him through thanksgiving, God keeps our minds in perfect peace.

The apostles often finished their letters with a blessing, imparting grace and peace to the believers. The most notable is surely Paul's encouragement to the Philippians, not to be anxious but to pray and let the 'peace of God that – passes all understanding, (AV) – that surpasses all comprehension, (NASB) – that transcends all understanding, (NIV) guard their hearts and **minds** in Christ Jesus. In the Amplified expansion of this verse we read – God's peace is to 'mount guard over your hearts **and minds.**' (Philippians 4:7). And from verse 8, in The Passion Translation, we read, 'So keep your thoughts continually fixed on all that is authentic and real . . . **Fasten your thoughts on every glorious work of God, praising Him always.**'

Activation . . .

Determine to always use thanksgiving to keep your mind 'stayed on' your Good, Good Father, in all the different circumstances of life and 'may the Lord of peace Himself give you peace at all times and in every way.' (2 Thessalonians 3:16).

DAY 342 | Thanksgiving that Changes the Way I see Life

Yesterday we were reflecting on the gift of God that is our imagination. That part of our mind that can be filled with ideas, thoughts and creativity. We can use it to fix our gaze on the Lord, so that we come into a place of peace. 'Peace, absolute peace surrounds those whose imaginations are consumed with you, they confidently trust in you.' (Isaiah 26:3, TPT). Equally imagination can lead us down dark paths and into much worry if it feeds on the lies of the enemy, or dwells on a world without God, and without faith.

Now this word that is translated as 'mind' or 'imagination' appears just nine times in the Old Testament. And these references are fascinating and very modern! In Genesis 6:5 and 8:21 we are told that the imagination, inclination, or thoughts in the hearts of men were evil. The important thing to realise is that this is telling us not just that men have evil thoughts, but that the whole framework of their thinking is evil. Evil thoughts happen within an evil framework. In Deuteronomy 31:21 God tells Moses that despite all the good He has done for the people they are 'developing an intent' (NASB) to turn away from Him. In 1 Chronicles 28:9 David tells his son Solomon that God knows the motives/intent/imagination behind our thoughts. Again it's not just the thoughts, it's what behind them driving them – the framework, imagination or intent, that is important.

The idea is of a structure, something that has been formed; something that mankind has made, a framework that they trust in. These passages seem to clarify that the framework or structure that we adopt becomes the reference point through which we view life. This framework can mould our thoughts, our values and our expectations. So if I have a socialist framework my thoughts and reactions to any situation will be framed by that perspective and value system. If I have a feminist philosophy, my thoughts and responses to daily events and people will be framed by that. Similarly if I am a convinced capitalist, or a republican, or a democrat and so forth.

If however I am a convinced God perspective person, believing that in everything Jesus is the Way, the Truth and the Life and that God is most definitely always loving and faithful (Psalm 117). And if I am convinced in the depth of my being of this, I will be looking at life, events, and people through that framework. This will then affect my thoughts on a daily basis. So it is great to have good and godly thoughts – not evil ones as in Genesis 6, but it is even better to have a surrounding framework, perspective and value system – a God lens – for my thoughts that looks at, and responds to daily life, from that perspective.

Jesus said, "Be careful. Be on your guard against the yeast of the Pharisees and the Sadducees", warning against both religious and political 'spirits'. He knows that the 'framework' we adopt, that we bond ourselves to, will start to frame our lives through that perspective. Our thinking will then be shaped by that philosophy and we become like the 'idols' that we make, i.e. those things that we value (worship?) and trust in. (See Psalm 115:8).

Surely that is what Isaiah 26:3 means when it talks of a mind, or imagination, stayed on the Lord – fixed on the Lord, even locked on. It means my mind is fixed, my glasses are firmly on my nose to see everything in life through the framework of who God is, what He has said, how trustworthy He is and much more beside. We can now see as we come to the end of our year of meditations that a lifestyle of thanksgiving will help to 'frame' how we view life. The more I am thanking and praising God for all He is, all He has done, all He has promised, the more I will be forming the framework, or perspective through which I view, and respond to all my life, my experiences and my expectations.

Activation ...

Take time to regularly soak yourself in God's word, consuming it and thanking Him that it is all true. He really is most wonderful, full of steadfast love, mercy, grace and faithfulness; then not only your thoughts, but the very framework, ideas, imaginations, structures and values of how you look at and respond to daily life events and people will be being changed. Thanksgiving gives you that framework (glasses) through which to view your life, God and the world. As an added bonus, thanksgiving also keeps cleaning those glasses afresh when they get smudged by the contrary ideas, thoughts and emotions being expressed all around us on a daily basis.

DAY 343 | Thanksgiving and Childlikeness

In Matthew 18:1-4 we read of the time when the disciples asked Jesus', "who is greatest in the kingdom of heaven?" Jesus stands a little child in the middle of them and says, "I tell you the truth, unless you change and become like little children, you will never enter the kingdom of Heaven. Therefore whoever humbles himself like this child is the greatest in the kingdom of Heaven." Now Jesus used a little child as the visual aid, not a teenager, probably not even an older primary school child, but a little one, and I fell to wondering, 'What is it about little children that Jesus was highlighting? What caused Him to make such an emphatic statement as "I tell you the truth..."?

I rather think it was trust that Jesus was highlighting. The kind of trust young children display before life events and traumas start to erode, even destroy the ability to trust. In fact it may be their readiness to trust so naturally that explains why early life experiences can have such a deep effect. Perhaps that is why Jesus warned (verses 5 and 6), about the serious consequences of causing a little child to sin, and thereby lose that innocent trust.

As I thought about this it resonated with our previous reflections. What is the hallmark of the man or woman who finds peace? It's the ability to have their mind (imagination) stayed and fixed on the Lord; why? 'because he **trusts** in you.' (Isaiah 26:3). There we have it! But 'familiarity' here can definitely 'breed contempt'. We can say 'Oh yes, yes, I know faith and trust are very important in the Christian life'. But have we grasped just **how** vital trust in the Lord is; how foundational and essential it is in the way that Jesus spoke about it that day? Do we realise that '**trust** in the Lord' is the framework, the paradigm, the foundational structure, the clean lens about which we wrote yesterday. The lens through which I need to see the whole of my life, all the daily events, all my relationships, all my hopes and fears, all my battles, and all of what I see of myself?

So here we have a paradox: In our journey with Jesus it feels like we need to go deeper and deeper in terms of **trust**ing the Lord, becoming more like little children, while at the same time we need to become more mature. 'Growing up into Christ in all things'. (see Ephesians 4:15). This Christian walk with the Lord certainly seems to have this wonderful twist in it! So how do we do this?

As you would by now expect, our greatest ally on this journey towards childlikeness coupled with maturity is 'giving thanks in all things.' (1 Thessalonians 5:18). The more I focus on all that I have to thank the Lord for, all He is, His character, His promises, His word, all He has done for me in salvation, last year, last week and yesterday, the more my trust in Him will grow. When I forget his benefits, things go downhill, but when I remember them with much thanksgiving trust and faith grow and I become like the centurion and the Canaanite woman who viewed Jesus through the lens of simple, straightforward but unwavering and powerful trust. Trust that astonished and thrilled Jesus!

We are called as Christians to 'grow in the grace and knowledge of our Lord and Saviour Jesus Christ.' (2 Peter 3:18), and so we need to guard against the voices of our modern, intellectual, scientific, rational age; those voices from the world, the media or even sadly from friends and other Christians, that say "It is far too simplistic to believe that God works in everything for my good as His child." (Romans 8:28). Voices, (even in our own heads) that look down on us for holding to our child-like faith, that the Lord is absolutely loving and powerful, and that He cares deeply for us in every aspect of our lives.

Activation . . .

Today make sure that you remember Jesus words, "I praise you Father, Lord of heaven and earth, because you have hidden these things from the wise and learned, and revealed them to little children. Yes Father, for this was your good pleasure." (Matthew 11:25-26). 'Little children' again! Refuse the voices that say, "It's more complicated than that, I am now wise and clever and grown up". Become like a little child, and be more simply committed to radical and persistent thanksgiving. Let your world view, be framed by simple childlike trust, that the Lord is utterly good, utterly loving, utterly faithful, utterly powerful and utterly wise. And that all of that goodness is directed at me, His very, very well loved child.

DAY 344 | Thanksgiving and Trust

Yesterday we were pondering Jesus' words to His disciples, "I tell you the truth, unless you change and become like little children you will never enter the kingdom of Heaven. Therefore whoever humbles himself like this child is the greatest in the kingdom of Heaven." (Matthew 18:1-4). We were looking at the child's ability to trust, and today we are going to look at how that ability to trust like a little child is linked to humbling ourselves.

A child's unspoilt ability to trust is there because the child perceives that the adults in his or her world are bigger, stronger, and wiser than they are. They will also trust because they feel themselves to be loved and therefore safe in the care of that adult. It is only when a child begins to perceive that there are dangers and difficulties in the world that others are unaware of, or unable to control and 'fix', that they begin to realise that they have to take care of themselves.

It can be a very humbling thing for a grown up person to reverse that process and learn to trust another adult. So for example in a hospital situation we all feel that vulnerability, as we make that decision to 'trust' the surgeon. When we fly, we make the decision to 'trust' the pilot, the engineers who maintain the plane and the air traffic control who guide the plane. We can do nothing but trust them all, (or maybe you, like me, put your trust in the angels who are watching over the whole procedure!) If we don't trust, we will be feeling very anxious, even unable to fly.

It is a humbling thing to have to trust someone else for my well being and safety, and to the extent that I manage to do that I feel peace. If I can't trust, then my anxiety levels rise. This, I think, is why anxiety among young children is on the rise. There are more and more situations where the adults in their lives are either untrustworthy, or have no power to guarantee their safety in different situations.

The converse should therefore be true for us as God's children as we grow and mature as Christians grasping more and more just how trustworthy our wonderful heavenly Father is. Our anxiety levels should be decreasing. Remember that Jesus said, 'Do not worry ... for your heavenly Father **knows** that you need them.' (Matthew 6:25-32). Which reminds me of a lovely

Christian friend I had many years ago who, whenever I shared any trouble or worry would say, "He **knows** Stella, He knows."

When I become a Christian, I embark on a journey whereby I am learning to 'trust' the Lord. Trusting Him to guide my choices and decisions, open the doors for my career, provide for me financially, care for me etc. etc. In fact I am learning to trust Him with my whole life. I am learning to 'trust' again like a little child because I now have a wonderful, totally faithful, totally loving and totally powerful Heavenly Father. If I don't humble myself and become more childlike in my faith and trust, I will find my anxiety levels increase and so the temptation to sin gets stronger.

This is because without a 'childlike trust' in the Lord, I will have to trust in my own abilities to sort life out. I am therefore more likely to become independent, make my own plans, go my own way, try to provide for my own needs. I may well even try to gain approval from God and others by my own efforts. Becoming a mature Christian, paradoxically involves becoming more humble as I become like a child seeking, and believing for, my heavenly Father's help and grace in every area of my life.

James tells us that, "God opposes the proud but gives grace to the humble." and then he encourages us with the words, 'Humble yourselves before the Lord, and He will lift you up.'(James 4:6,10). This is so contrary to how the world thinks. In the Kingdom of God it is good not to be self sufficient. It is good rather to be like a little child, to take Abba's (Daddy's) hand, trust Him and receive His help and grace at all times.

Receiving this grace on a daily basis involves three things, i) Being humble enough to acknowledge my need and ask for help ii) Believing that Father, Son, and Holy Spirit delight to make all grace abound to me so that in all things at all times, having all that I need, I will abound in every good work. (See 2 Corinthians 9:8), and iii) **giving thanks in faith**, like a child accepting help. These three steps give us a sure way to appropriate all the 'grace gifts' that I need.

Activation . . .

In every situation in which you find yourself, grow in childlike trust today as you humble yourself, **give thanks, and receive** all that you need moment by moment.

DAY 345 | Thanksgiving and Humility

Over the past few days we have been considering the links between childlikeness, trust and humility. Without childlike trust in the Lord, I can become anxious. I doubt His care and His ability to lead and guide me as an incredibly loving Father would, and so I take hold of things myself, I try to sort my life out as best I can, independent of His Fatherly guidance, protection and direction. This can then lead to sin because independence means that I start to do what is right, or what I think is needed, from my own perspective.

In fact this is probably the difference between David and Saul. King Saul, when faced with Samuel's delay, was afraid of the people and so he made his own plan to fulfill his religious duty to try and please God. (See 1 Samuel 13:1-14 and 1 Samuel 15:20-24). David, on the other hand, refused man's advice about how to defeat Goliath and trusted God saying, "The Lord who delivered me from the paw of the lion and the paw of the bear will deliver me from the hand of this Philistine." (1 Samuel 17:37). He placed his trust firmly in the Lord.

We read that "... the righteous will live by his faith –" (Habakkuk 2:4), and that, 'everything that does not come from faith is sin.' (Romans 14:23). So relying on myself, is not always a good scene when it comes to the Kingdom of God. And if self reliance moves me out of a place of 'faith', and of childlike trust, then it will probably lead to sin.

In Proverbs 3: 5 Solomon tells us to, '**Trust** in the Lord with **all** your heart and lean not to your own understanding; in all your ways acknowledge him and he will make your paths straight. **Do not be wise in your own eyes**; fear the Lord, and shun evil.' And in the kingdom, we are told, God did not call many who were wise by human standards.' But in fact God said, "I will destroy the wisdom of the wise; the intelligence of the intelligent I will frustrate." (Have a read through 1 Corinthians 1:19-30).

Becoming wise in our own eyes repeats the original sin whereby Adam and Eve ate of the tree of the knowledge of good and evil. (See Genesis 3:5,6). Becoming mature in the Lord, becoming a wise woman or man of God, is about growing in childlike trust, so that when He prompts me to give more that I think I can, I trust, like Abraham, in my Jehovah-Jireh who will provide for me. (Genesis 22:13,14). If He calls me to go somewhere, or do something that I feel unable to do, and there seems no way through, I can obey because He is the God who made a way through the Red sea for the Israelites, and He will do that for me too. (Exodus 14:29).

When I am faced with overwhelming odds, like Joshua taking the children of Israel into the Promised Land, I remember that God said, "Be strong and courageous. Do not be terrified; do not be discouraged, for the Lord your God will be with you wherever you go." (Joshua 1:9). Then, as I go in childlike trust, I can follow His lead, even if it seems as if it is not the most obvious way to win the battle, in the same way that walking around the city walls for seven days needed some trust on Joshua's part.

Martin Smith wrote a beautiful song a while back now, 'Here I am, humbled by your Majesty'[1], the chorus of which speaks to me of the power of humble trust. It goes 'Majesty, Majesty, your grace has found me just as I am, empty handed but alive in your hands.' Being humble before the Majesty of God, makes me aware of my own lack, but also of His magnificence, and therefore of all that is mine in Christ, including His wisdom.

That amazing statement that Paul makes, 'I can do all things through Him who strengthens me,' (Philippians 4:13, NASB), then becomes one that I can make too. It is not a proud statement, but the statement of a humble child of God who, recognising their own emptiness, is able to increasingly trust their Heavenly Father in all circumstances. Life then becomes one opportunity after another to grow in experiencing the 'Life of Christ' flowing through me, leading and guiding with the wisdom that is from above.

Activation . . .

In Proverbs 3:5 (the verse quoted above) the word translated, 'acknowledge' him is actually the more intimate word 'know' him. The same word used as Adam 'knew' Eve (Genesis 4:1, AMP). If I am to walk 'humbly with my God' trusting Him with my whole heart, then I need to 'know' Him in a very intimate way. This intimacy will grow as I give myself to thanksgiving that the powerful God of heaven is actually living in me, then in all my circumstances I will find it easier to trust in His wisdom, provision, and enabling grace. And, like a trusting child, I will be astounded at His goodness and care for me.

DAY 346 | Thanksgiving, Rest and Action

On previous days we have written about how thanksgiving is an important ingredient in the 'life of rest'. The 'rest of faith', about which we read in Hebrews chapter 4. It resonates with Jesus' call to come to Him and find rest for our souls. (Matthew 11:28,29). Thanksgiving is also a huge ingredient in contentment, and Paul reminds us that godliness with contentment is great gain, (1 Timothy 6:6). So thanksgiving is an important ingredient in both rest and contentment; from the enormous faith issues – He died for me on the cross, forgave me everything, gave me life, lives in me daily and promises me eternity in His presence – to the so called 'small' daily provisions – I have food today, clothing, a home and so much more.

Recently while chatting to a visitor about gratitude I got to asking myself whether gratitude, such a healthy attitude to have, could sometimes lead to passivity, a sort of fatalism, or belief in 'karma', expressed in this way: "The world is the way it is, what 'will be' will be, so the best way to live in it is to notice and be grateful for everything I can." Now while gratitude is a tremendous attitude to have I wondered, after talking to my visitor, if there could be a problem if there was only gratitude and no imperative, or hunger to seek for more, to ask for help, or for something different; the kind of hunger that could take my visitor from passive acceptance to seeking the Lord. I began to wonder if there could be a Christian version of this passivity. "Whatever happens is God's will, I will submit to it and be grateful and 'rest' in it." But is this biblical, or a kind of Christian fatalism?

Jesus said. "Blessed are those who hunger and thirst for righteousness, for they shall be filled." (Matthew 5:6). Hungering and thirsting sounds like I don't want things to stay the same and I am very keen for things to be different! "Ask (and keep on asking) and it will be given to you . . ." (Matthew 7:7) Here and in other places Jesus clearly seemed to teach His disciples not to accept things as inevitable, but to ask, knock and seek persistently for more, for change, or for different. (see Luke 18:1-8).

When we look into this further, it would seem that Jesus' life was filled with people asking Him for more (often healing and health) – and He was always blessed by their asking – even when the original request wasn't on the 'right' lines! (Matthew 15:21-28). Jesus reminds us in His conversation with Philip that He was just like His Father, (John 14:9). Jesus taught us that He and His Father were, and are, delighted to be asked for help, both for what we need and want for ourselves, and for others also. (See John 16:23,24.)

So how does healthy, biblical thanksgiving bring these two truths about 'rest and contentment', and 'hunger and asking', together? Well let's start with Philippians 4:6,7, where Paul encourages us, 'Do not be anxious about anything, but in everything, by prayer and petition, with thanksgiving, present your requests to God. And the peace of God which transcends all understanding, will guard your hearts and your minds in Christ Jesus.' Asking for more with, or through, the portal of thanksgiving, meets the grace of God, and with that grace comes peace, rest and contentment.

You could say that Hebrews 4, where the importance of entering into God's rest is strongly emphasised, approaches it from the other direction. Here it is the rest of faith, believing that God is who He says He is, that He keeps all His promises, that He loves me to bits, is caring for me and working everything for my good, that will encourage me to pray and ask for that for which I am hungering and thirsting. Thanksgiving is here such a powerful element in keeping us in that place of rest and contentment, but then from that place of faith filled rest we can move into asking, action and obedience, and of course it was faith that led all those people to hungrily chase after Jesus for their healing.

Activation . . .

Faith in the goodness, love, listening ear and power of our Lord will lead us to hungrily pray for His interventions – from a place of the 'rest' of faith. Being thankful becomes the central anchor point that keeps me at rest whilst hungrily asking, seeking and knocking in faith. So let thanksgiving be a powerful and central ingredient in helping you to live with the paradox/ mystery of being at rest and content in your life with the Lord and yet full of hunger and faith for 'the more' that God always has in store.

DAY 347 | Thanksgiving that Multiplies our Resources

We read in the gospels of the miracle feeding of the five thousand from five loaves and two fish, and we need to note that this miracle was preceded by the Lord lifting up His eyes to heaven and giving thanks. (Matthew 14:17-21). The same thing happened when He fed the four thousand. The thanksgiving that preceded these miracles was a wonderful sign of the faith and confidence that Jesus had in His heavenly Father's willingness and power to provide for these hungry people.

Prior to this happening one of the disciples had suggested to Jesus that the crowd be sent away to the surrounding villages in order to be able to get some food. Jesus' reply was, "They do not need to go away. **You give them something to eat.**" The disciples then looked at what they had got and quite reasonably replied "We have here only five loaves of bread and two fish." And so Jesus says, **"Bring them here to me". He gives thanks** and then lets the disciples give out food they didn't think they had.

I wonder how often you and I have seen a need to help someone, or an opportunity to bless someone, looked at our own resources and thought, "Nope! What I've got is just not enough." "I've not enough time for this conversation". "I've not enough money to give for this need." "I've not enough patience to be kind in this situation." "I've not enough faith to pray for this person." "I've not enough confidence to step out and do ... X ... Y or ... Z." "I've not enough knowledge to defend my faith." etc. etc. Fill in the gaps, where you may be aware of your own areas of 'lack'.

Well my thought today is that **thanksgiving has a clear link to supernatural multiplication.** I think that Jesus modeled something for us on these two occasions when He fed the crowds, and it was this. If we **'bring what we have to Jesus'**, and join Him in raising our hearts and our eyes to heaven, and **give thanks for what we might see as meagre resources**, then we may well experience a miracle as we go ahead and give what we thought that we didn't have.

The central ingredient in these miracles is the giving of thanks. It is more than just giving the little I have to God. That's a great start but as I give what I have, and give thanks, I am raising my eyes to heaven and releasing my faith. Jesus gave thanks **before the miracle because He knew that it was going to happen.**

It reminds me of the widow at Zarephath, who had so little, only enough in fact for one more meal for her and her son during a time of drought. Elijah tells her to first make, from this small amount of flour, a cake of bread and then He says **"bring it to me"** (1 Kings 17:7-16). She does this extraordinary faith filled action, effectively giving to God all that she and her son have to keep them alive as she feeds this 'man of God'. Then the miracle happens and she finds that God provides her with flour and oil for bread, every day, until the drought ends.

In all areas of life practical, emotional, and spiritual, let us turn our 'lack' into an opportunity for a miracle. We don't need to know how the miracle will happen, but we will grow in faith for a supernatural lifestyle as we **bring to Jesus what little we have,** of our strength, patience, love and kindness, energy, time, wisdom etc, **give Him thanks** and then in faith 'pour out' what we have.

Activation . . .

Whenever you feel a lack, in whatever area of life, **bring what you have to the Lord,** and lay it at His feet. As you offer it to Him, raise your eyes to heaven **and give thanks**. As you give, what you consider to be your meagre resources, **with thanksgiving**, I think you will see the miracles happen. You will speak out in faith and find that what you have to say is good; your prayer however short and simple will be effective; you will find your love, patience and kindness increasing, your financial resources replenished unexpectedly, and your energy renewed. As you give, maybe others will give too, and more needs will be met through the multiplication of thanksgiving.

DAY 348 | Thanksgiving and the Love Languages of Heaven

I was thinking yesterday about the mysterious prayer that Paul prayed for the Ephesians! **'that you, being rooted and established in love, may have power, together with all the saints, to grasp how wide and long and how high and deep is the love of Christ, and to know this love that surpasses knowledge – that you may be filled to the measure of all the fullness of God.'** (Ephesians 3:17-19). It tells us that there is much of God's love that is beyond our comprehension, but that we are invited to explore, or push into, His love more and more. God's love is clearly unfathomable and yet is something into which we can go ever deeper.

I remember one time as a young Christian, asking the Lord to show me His love. I wanted a onetime overwhelming experience that would last me for the rest of my life, after which I would never doubt again!! The Holy Spirit seemed to be saying to me, "It's there in the bible. My love has been demonstrated on the cross. There is nothing more to say." I think the Lord wanted me to be 'rooted and established' in the facts of what His love had accomplished for me on the cross rather than on a one off 'experience'. I was a little disappointed but I subsequently realised that any experience that He gave me would not necessarily last. The next day, next week or next year it would be easy to think back and wonder, "Was that really the Lord? Did I imagine that? Why have those feelings gone now, has the Lord's love gone too?" In other words experiences alone without being rooted in the truth of God's Word, would leave me like any mystic, (from any religion) vulnerable to doubts and in need of further experiences.

I needed, back then as a young Christian, to understand that finding out how much God loves me is a lifetime's journey. His love is unbounded and limitless. This explains why my 'one off lifetime experience' to settle the matter, was not a good idea. God loves us enough to want for us to grow and develop an understanding of His love, through all the different seasons of life; both in the peaceful and the turbulent times; in the context of His body and when I am walking with Him on my own. David understood this, and wrote the 23rd Psalm. No wonder he was described as 'a man after God's own heart.' (see 1 Samuel 13:14). So how then do we get to 'know this love of God that surpasses knowledge'? Now I believe God does give feelings and experiences, and they are good, as is understanding truth with my mind, but I am now thinking that our wonderful Heavenly Father is an expert in love languages as well, and so He will use many different languages of love to help us explore the height, depth, length and breadth of His love.

In Gary Chapman's book, 'The 5 Love Languages'[1] he explains how we all have different ways of expressing and receiving love. He delineates five main 'Love Languages', (although there may be more). They are i) Words of affirmation, ii) Quality time, iii) Physical touch, iv) Acts of service, and v) The giving of gifts. I got to thinking how God uses all of these languages. He knows what will reach our hearts. First and foremost we need to be rooted and grounded in the truth of 1 John 3:16, – **'This is how we know what love is: Jesus Christ laid down His life for us.'** then I believe God also delights to show us His love daily, taking us deeper into His love by using all those love languages, and others too, that are tailored to our individual personality.

Activation . . .

So remember when He gives you 'Words of Affirmation' **receive them with thanksgiving.** DON'T dismiss them! He will give you endless 'Quality Time' to talk to Him, and He will listen to you, and hear what is in your hearts. **Be thankful** that you can pray at anytime and anywhere. He will 'Touch' your body and mind with health and healing, and with renewal and refreshment, as you come and 'wait on Him' (Isaiah 40:28-31). So wait on Him with **a grateful heart** and you will prove this scripture to be true. He does so many amazing 'Acts of Service' for you. Learn to recognise these lovely acts of pure kindness, as well as His daily practical care, **and be thankful** so that, at all costs, you resist the urge to dismiss these things as coincidences. Similarly accept 'His Gifts' **with great gratitude,** and you'll find other gifts will come your way very soon. Let **'thanksgiving'** be the key to your exploration of God's love, 'the height, length, depth and breadth of it', and you will discover more and more of His endless love every day.

DAY 349 | Thanksgiving and God's Faithfulness

One of the most wonderful ways in which God demonstrates His love to us is through His faithfulness. Even the notion of 'faithfulness' is something that only a God created sentient being can understand. This is because faithfulness is not about instinct, or feelings, but about choice. Faithfulness is embedded in God's character, and should you talk to an atheist; someone who actually believes that everything came out of nothing; that gases and particles randomly coalesced to form our universe, and that living beings like you and I evolved from those chemicals, they will have no explanation for there being anything like real 'love' and certainly no explanation for 'faithfulness'.

Because love and faithfulness are embedded in the character of our wonderful creator God we, as beings created in His image, get it! We know if someone is being faithful or not; we know what it means to be faithful ourselves. And interestingly, even in our amoral world, no matter what people say, the experience of someone being unfaithful to them is quite devastating. This is because faithfulness is a beautiful and wonderful quality upon which all good relationships are built. It is enshrined in the marriage vows, and underpins all covenant relationships.

I love the dramatic scene described in Revelation 19:11-13, 'I saw heaven standing open and there before me was a white horse, whose rider is called 'Faithful and True'... He is dressed in a robe dipped in blood, and his name is the Word of God'. Our Jesus – our Saviour – has taken on, for all eternity, the name 'Faithful and True'; He is God's 'word' to us for all time, and remember, He is faithful even when we aren't. 'If we are faithless he will remain faithful, for he cannot disown himself'. (2 Timothy 2:13).

David, in Psalm 36:5, links together 'love' and 'faithfulness'. He writes, 'Your love, O Lord, reaches to the heavens, your faithfulness to the skies.' This is just a wonderfully poetic way of saying that there is nothing to touch the enormity of God's love and faithfulness. God's love and faithfulness literally tower over everything else we can imagine. Not surprisingly then it is often our trust in God's faithfulness that the enemy attacks. Perhaps it is because he knows that relying on God's faithfulness makes us dangerous to his plans to destroy God's Kingdom on the earth.

If we listen to Moses handing over leadership to Joshua, when the Promised Land lay before them and many battles lay ahead, we will hear these words, "Be strong and courageous. Do not be afraid or terrified because of them for the Lord your God goes with you; **he will never leave you or forsake you.**" (Deuteronomy 31:6-8). It is also these words that the writer to the Hebrews quotes as he encourages those Hebrew Christians to press on with God in times of difficulty, and in the Amplified Bible we get the full force of those words, with the emphasis of a triple negative.

'... be satisfied with your present [circumstances and with what you have]; for He (God) Himself has said. I will not in any way fail you, nor give you up, nor leave you without support. [I will not], [I will] not, [I will] not in any degree leave you helpless *nor* forsake, *nor* let you down (relax my hold on you)! [Assuredly not!] (Hebrews 13:5, AMP). And our response to that is **'So we say with confidence, "The Lord is my helper; I will not be afraid. What can man do to me?"** (Hebrews 13:6, NIV).

When I am faced with challenges to my faith, and I am tempted to doubt the Lord's commitment to me, thankfulness will drive away all my doubts concerning His faithfulness. As I thank God for the truth of that scripture; those words first said by Moses over 3,000 years ago, and then repeated by the writer to the Hebrews some 2,000 years ago, and then remind myself as I thank God that, 'Jesus Christ is the same yesterday and today and forever.' (Hebrews 13:8), I can rest my faith on who He is, and not on who I am or what I am trying to do.

Activation ...

Make sure that you keep thanking God for this truth, and stay connected to this core attribute of God. Meditating on and thanking Him for His faithfulness daily, is a key part of 'building myself up in my most holy faith...' and of '... keeping myself in God's love' (Jude verse 20).

DAY 350 | Thanksgiving and Light

It's that time of year again when we lose so many hours of natural light and then, suddenly, we see many different kinds of light springing up all around us. Lights and Christmas seem go together in our world. Christmas lights coming as a welcome contrast to the decorations of Halloween a few weeks earlier. Sadly not too many around us seem to be looking for the real 'Light of the World.' Perhaps it's because they haven't yet 'seen' who that is.

The arrival of Jesus, 'The Light of the World', born into the Jewish nation, was prophesied by Isaiah in that famous passage, 'The people walking in darkness have seen **a great light**; on those living in the land of the shadow of death **a light** has dawned.' (Isaiah 9:2). A subsequent prophesy about the Messiah in Isaiah 42:6 reads, 'I will keep you and make you to be a covenant for the people and **a light** for the Gentiles.' It's a declaration that His mission now includes all of us, Jew and Gentile!!

In the New Testament it becomes even clearer that Jesus came as the 'bringer of light'. This is not physical light of course, but spiritual light; light that leads to real life. In John's gospel, chapter 1:4,5, we read, 'In Him was life, and that life was the **light** of men. The **light shines** in the darkness, but the darkness has not understood it.' Quite simply put, '**God is light**; in Him there is no darkness at all.' (1 John 1:5), and if we live by His light, we also have the abundant life of which Jesus spoke, (John 10:10). We carry His 'light' and 'life'; the very things that our darkening world needs.

As we were worshipping this morning we sang a lovely chorus based on the middle verses from Psalm 36:7-9, 'How precious, is Your loving kindness, O God! And the children of men take refuge in the shadow of your wings. They drink their fill of the abundance of Your house. And you give them to drink of the river of Your delights. For with You is the fountain of Life; **in your light do we see light**. With you is the fountain of Life; **in Your light we see light**.'

What a wonderful promise to us living in a world where there is increasing spiritual, as well as natural, darkness all around. Jesus declared such a wonderful truth when He said, "I am the **Light** of the world. Whoever follows me will never walk in darkness, but will have the **light of life**." (John 8:12). Then it occurred to me that, like any light, the closer you get to it the more easily you can 'see'. Having 'Light', living an 'abundant life', and 'drinking from the river of delights', it all gets stronger, and more real, as we draw daily closer to Jesus.

The apostle Peter wrote this statement to some early Christians, who were living in a very pagan environment, 'But you are a chosen race, a royal priesthood, a dedicated nation, [God's] own purchased, special people, **that you may set forth the wonderful deeds *and* display the perfections of Him who called you out of darkness into His marvelous light.**' (1 Peter 2:9, AMP). We have been translated from the dominion of Darkness into the Kingdom of the Son, (Colossians 1:13), in order that we might shine that **light** into the world around us.

If we want to shine, to be **'light'** in our dark world, it's quite simple really, we just need to keep close to Jesus. If we stay close we will have lots to share of His wonderful deeds with those living around us who are still in 'darkness'. If we go back to Psalm 36, we can see that the promises written there about 'light' and 'life' are to those who 'find refuge under the shadow of His wing'. Now that is close! And so we come back to 'thanksgiving' because in my experience the more grateful I am to the Lord – that He is **'my light and my Salvation'** – the closer we become.

The Lord is always with me, my Emmanuel, but I can hold Him at arms length by my doubts and my fears, or by my independence. But if I am filled with gratitude for all that He has saved me from, and for the way He leads and guides me through life; if I can stay thankful for the **'Light'** He has given me and the **'Life'** He has poured into me, and stay thankful for all those times that He has been my refuge, even when I didn't realise I was in need of one, then I find myself drawing ever closer to Him in my spirit.

Activation ...

Let your thanksgiving draw you close to the Lord today and Isaiah 60:19 will increasingly become your testimony in a darkening world.

*'The sun will no longer be needed to brighten your day, nor the moon to shine at night, for Yahweh will be your **unfailing light**; and your God will be your glory!'* TPT.

DAY 351 | Thanksgiving and Giving

We are reminded at Christmas time that, at the heart of Christianity, there is a 'Giving God'; One who loves to give. The new life that we have in Christ all starts in the heart of our 'Giving God', who 'so loved the world that He **gave** His only Son . . .' (John 3:16). It is reasonable then to suppose that as we grow to be more like Him we will find ourselves wanting to be 'a **giver**' like Him.

At Christmas, a special time for giving, we look carefully for presents to **give** to family and friends, to those we love, (or with whom we want to stay in good relationship!!). We might also **give** some extra to a charity at this time of year, to the homeless, or those dealing with those in crisis at Christmas. In fact it's not that hard to **give** to those we love and to those we feel deserve our gifts. God's **giving** is, however, at another level.

We read that, 'because of his great love for us, God, who is rich in mercy, made us alive with Christ even when we were dead in our transgressions . . .' (Ephesians 2:4). That is to say, when we had done nothing, and could do nothing, to earn His gift. When there was nothing in us to deserve it, God had great pleasure in **giving** to us, unilaterally, lavishly and sacrificially, out of His huge compassion, mercy and generosity. (Ephesians 1:3-8).

Unlike any other faith or world religion, where the god or gods have to be appeased and where blessing and favour have to be earned, at the heart of our faith is a wonderful Being who loves and gives Himself for us, even before we know Him. Then Jesus Himself says to us that **we** should aim to be like our Heavenly Father who, 'causes his sun to rise on the evil and the good, and sends rain on the righteous and the unrighteous.' (Matthew 5:45).

Jesus is saying that, in order to be like our Father in heaven we need to have a heart to 'give' to those outside our close circle, and to those to whom we would not naturally be drawn. He asked the question, 'If you love those who love you what reward will you get? . . . What are you doing more than others? Do not even the pagans do that? Be perfect, therefore, as your heavenly Father is perfect.' (Matthew 5:46,47).

'When the Son of Man comes in His glory' in order to judge the world, the ones who are welcomed in to take their inheritance aren't primarily noticed by the way they preached, evangelised or prophesied; they aren't pointed out for their faith, or the miracles and healings that they have done, they are rather commended because they **gave** to those who could not return the favour. 'For I was hungry and you **gave** me something to eat, I was thirsty and you **gave** me something to drink ...'. You **gave** me hospitality, you **gave** me clothes, you **gave** me dignity, you **gave** some comfort, you **gave** some help in time of need (in prison or trouble). (Matthew 25:31-35).

Jesus also said, 'It is more blessed to give than to receive.' (Acts 20:35), and so He instructed His followers, 'Heal the sick, raise the dead, cleanse those who have leprosy, drive out demons. Freely have you received freely **give**.' (Matthew 10:8). So whether we are giving unreturnable kindnesses, or using the more dramatic spiritual gifts, it is always to be with a heart of 'freely giving'; not performing, earning anyone's approval, or looking for reward.

In order to be like our Heavenly Father we need to 'Live to Give', not just at Christmas. We can **give** way on the motorway, **give** a hand to someone who is struggling at the checkout, **give** a good tip to the waiter, **give** a kind word, or a smile; **give** a word of encouragement, **give** someone our time and skills, etc. etc. And, if we are to be like our Father, we need to **give**, not just to the deserving, but to bless those we will never see again, those who don't deserve anything, and those who have nothing to give back.

Activation ...

Let thankfulness for all your undeserved blessings create a culture of giving in your heart; a giving lifestyle and so be released to live generously and sacrificially. As you thank the Lord for all He has **given you**, you will be like the child who, having been given a very large bag of sweets, finds it so much easier to share than when he just has two or three sweets in his pocket.

Thank Him for every opportunity to give and give again, becoming more and more like Him in all that you do. Your eyes will be opened to see those opportunities not as duty, or 'do I have to give?', but as a 'Wow! **Thank you Lord for another opportunity where I get to give just like you.**'

DAY 352 | Thanksgiving and Giving God our Cares

Yesterday we were meditating on the truth that, since we have a '**Giving** God', we will increasingly become generous '**Givers**' ourselves, just like Him. Now we probably know that sometimes it is hard to '**give**' to others when we are actually carrying a lot of stuff ourselves. That is to say that, when we are carrying heavy burdens that weigh us down and that preoccupy us, it is sometimes hard to notice those opportunities to '**give**' to others. If we do notice them, we can still feel worn out with our own 'stuff' and that we have nothing left to **give**!

It seems to me that in order to be able to be a big '**giver**' in life, we need first of all to **give** ourselves fully to the Lord, which includes being able to **give** our burdens to Him. I think Peter knew this because he wrote to his friends, who were probably having a tough time, 'Humble yourselves, therefore, under God's mighty hand, that he may lift you up in due time. Cast all your anxiety on Him because He cares for you.' (1 Peter 5:6,7).

David, a man who went through many storms and trials, likewise encourages us by writing, many, many years before Christ, 'Cast your cares on the Lord and he will sustain you; he will never let the righteous fall.' (Psalm 55:22). If we are to be free in ourselves, in order to be able to notice and **give** to others, if we are to be 'care **free**' and not 'care **full**', we are going to need to develop that skill of **casting**, or deliberately and actively **giving**, those same cares to the Lord and then letting go of them.

I think many of us have our 'cares' on a bungee rope tied around our waist. We do come to the Lord and give them to Him but, somehow, we don't let them go, and they bounce back into our minds/lives as soon as we leave our place of prayer and get back to the business of life. This could be because we are still trying to work things out for ourselves, or because we don't fully trust the Lord to sort things out as we would like Him too. In a way it doesn't matter why we don't fully give our cares to the Lord, but it does matter that we do learn to do so.

The Amplified Bible expands the last part of 1 Peter 5:7 like this. 'Casting the whole of your care (all your anxieties, all your worries, all your concerns, **once and for all**) on Him, for He cares for you affectionately and cares about you watchfully.' It's that 'once and for all' phrase that challenges me. So how do we do that? How do we fully let things go to Him and refuse to keep pulling them back onto our own shoulders again.

Yes. You guessed it. We stand on His word and we stay in thankfulness that He has heard us. We thank Him that He cares for us. We thank Him that His mighty hand will lift us up in due time; that he will sustain us and not let us fall. Thanksgiving for these truths, I believe, 'cuts' the bungee rope between us and our worries, and that so pleases the Lord. It's an amazing and wonderful thing that the Lord wants our cares; that He wants us to be 'care **free**'. Above all else He wants our trust, and that will be demonstrated in our ability to **give** Him our worries. He wants us to **give** Him **everything** that would weigh us down and take away our capacity for **giving** to others.

Activation . . .

Set your heart today to become 'care **free**' so that you can start on (or continue) your journey towards being a 'big **giver**' in life.

If the bungee rope connecting you to your burdens seems tough. be persistent in your thanksgiving and also find those promises that will help you to 'cut through it'; promises that address your specific cares.

You can also give thanks for the way He has taken care of you in the past, by keeping a note book recording your own previous testimony. This can be a good way of helping you to remember – when fresh cares come along – that you have a very, very faithful God.

DAY 353 | Thanksgiving and the Heavenly Beings!

Quite often in our daily readings we have been looking at the benefit that staying in a place of thanksgiving brings to us in our everyday lives. Today I want to focus on what happens in the heavenly realms when we give thanks. We know from 1 Chronicles 16:41,42, and 2 Chronicles 5:12-14 (see Days 324 and 325), that thanksgiving was an important ingredient in the Temple worship and that when the priests did what had been commanded, singing, **'give thanks to the Lord, "for His love endures forever."** the glory of God fell in the temple, (which was at that time His dwelling place on the earth). We are told that the weight of that glory was such that the priests could not continue with their service.

God specifically gave them that simple song to sing and showed His delight, when they sang it, by coming among them with His power and glory. So can we conclude then that thanksgiving is one of the languages of heaven? I believe so. I believe that every time we give thanks we honour Jesus. Every time we show our gratitude to Him, all of heaven rejoices because Jesus and His sacrifice are acknowledged and greatly appreciated. We are grateful to be God's children because Jesus went to the cross. We are so glad that we have a good God and we are so glad for all the benefits that this confers on us. (Psalm 103:1-5).

Our thanksgiving gives great joy in the heavenly realm to Jesus, to our Heavenly Father and to the beautiful Holy Spirit. So what of the other inhabitants of heaven, the angels? As we look through the bible they are constantly present and active in our world. They communicate between heaven and earth, bringing messages from God and acting on His behalf for His people. They too are exhorted, by the psalmist, to praise Him like us. 'Praise him all his angels, praise him all his heavenly hosts.' (Psalm 148:2). John when he was taken into heaven in the spirit, heard 'the voice of many angels numbering thousands upon thousands and ten thousand times ten thousand.' around the throne, (Revelation 5:11). What an incredible sound and what joy they must be experiencing in heaven as they sing, just awestruck, at what He has done for us.

We know that 'when God brings His firstborn Son into the world He says, "Let all God's angels worship Him." (Hebrews 1:6). We also know that they rejoice together whenever anyone becomes a Christian, (Luke 15:10). They see so much more clearly than us what God has done for us through Jesus, and I believe they just love it when we catch on and give our praise and thanks to Him. I believe that they don't just worship and give thanks before the throne but they join us on earth when we give thanks. They are drawn to gratitude, praise and worship.

If the angel armies love to hear our expressed gratitude, then it is also true that Satan and his angels of darkness hate it. I believe that they particularly hate it when we give thanks and use the powerful name of Jesus. Gratitude, giving honour, thanks and praise to Jesus is the last thing that Satan wants to hear coming from our lips. It drives him away, so he does all he can to silence us. Remember that God says "He who sacrifices thank offerings honours me, and he prepares a way so that I may show him the salvation of God." (Psalm 50:23). Our 'thank offerings', particularly those 'sacrificial ones' change the atmosphere and make way for the Lord to show us His way in our lives.

Activation . . .

Today take these thoughts as a fresh incentive to stay thankful, knowing that it delights your Heavenly Father's heart; it causes great joy among the angels **and** drives away your enemy. Charles Wesley grasped this reality and penned some wonderful lines in his Carol, 'Hark the Herald Angels Sing.'[1] Remember the wonderful crescendo of the last verse, 'Sing choirs of angels, sing in exultation, sing all you citizens of heaven above.' Don't let those lines be a narrative of what happened 2,000 years ago, but let your gratitude to God cause the angels great joy and give them more reason to 'visit' the earth, here and now in the twenty first century.

DAY 354 | Thanksgiving and 'Storms'

Many of our cards at Christmas speak of 'Peace', and rightly so because Christmas is the celebration of the coming of Jesus the 'Prince of Peace' (Isaiah 9:6). We genuinely want to bless our friends and family, Christian and non Christian, with 'Peace'. The problem is that Jesus, the Prince of Peace, came into a very troubled world and for many of us those good wishes for 'Peace' come likewise into troublesome life circumstances. Jesus came to earth and walked through life at a politically and socially turbulent time. He also faced much opposition personally and spiritually, and yet He walked with peace and dignity, in complete harmony with His Heavenly Father, in the power of the Holy Spirit.

We too are living in 'stormy' times economically, politically, and culturally because of the immense shifts that are taking place in our society and our world. And that is before we mention any 'storms' that people might be facing in their personal lives, their families; their finances, or their health and well being. There are also the spiritual storms as the struggle between the Kingdom of God and the kingdom of darkness intensifies. I believe that, however much of a stretch it may seem to be, God's plan in bringing us into His Kingdom at this time is so that we, by His grace, can also walk with His peace through all the trials and ups and downs of life.

The interesting thing about the storms recorded for us in the bible, is how often God uses them to achieve His purposes. For example Jonah eventually got to do God's will (however reluctantly) (Jonah 3:3); Paul got to prophesy safety to his shipmates and had great opportunities to demonstrate the power of God in Malta. (Acts 27:13-28:10). Jesus demonstrated His power over the elements, (Luke 8:22-25), and Peter got to have a big adventure and a great lesson in faith. (Matthew 14:28-31). The fact is God's presence trumps any storm, whether it is a storm of our own making, a hurricane sent by the enemy, world events, or something that God has Himself set up.

Jesus was clear with His disciples, "In this world you will have trouble. But take heart! I have overcome the world." (John16:33). And "Peace I leave with you; my peace I give you. I do not give to you as the world gives. Do not let your hearts be troubled and do not be afraid." (John 14:27). So how do we travel through life, or through a turbulent season of life, with peace in our hearts? Clearly the answer lies in knowing that the Prince of Peace is with us in the storm, and not just watching us from afar.

We wrote some weeks ago about the eagle and its ability to soar above any turbulence or storm as it caught the thermals. We quoted Isaiah 40:31 where, we are told that, 'those who wait upon the Lord shall renew their strength; they shall mount up with wings as eagles; they shall run, and not be weary, and they shall walk and not faint.' (AV). We spoke then of renewal and refreshment, but today I want to revisit that verse, because I believe it can also help us as we endeavour to walk in peace through all the various storms of life, like our wonderful King Jesus.

The phrase 'wait upon the Lord' is not, as we have said before, an inactive verb. It is not like waiting in for a parcel to be delivered, or waiting for a bus or train. Waiting upon the Lord, carries the sense of being 'entwined' with the Lord, (see Psalm 25:5 TPT footnote), and it implies great intimacy. David writes, 'no king is saved by the size of his army; no warrior escapes by his great strength ... We wait in hope for the Lord; he is our help and our shield.' (Psalm 33:16,20). Deliverance comes as we entwine our hearts with His.

When Peter was walking on the water, the wind and the waves were not a problem for God, but when Peter looked and saw them he got fearful and began to sink. The lovely thing about that story was that Jesus was right there, put out His hand and drew (entwined) Peter close to Him, and back into the boat. (Matthew 14:28-33). As we entwine our hearts with God's heart His wrap around presence surrounds us. It is like Jesus' invitation to the weary and heavy laden to come close to Him; to take His yoke, learn from Him and thereby find rest for their souls. (See Matthew 11:28).

Activation ...

In whatever 'storm' you might be currently facing, wait on the Lord where it's peaceful and still. I believe we can always start that process of 'waiting upon Him', or 'entwining our heart' with His, by giving Him thanks for His presence. Giving thanks will always turn your eyes from the wind and the waves that you are facing and onto Jesus, and when you know that He is that close you will find, like Peter, that your peace returns.

DAY 355 | Gratitude and Christmas

Last Christmas I was so sad as I walked around a garden centre looking at all the Christmas decorations and paraphernalia, because I could only find one small 'nativity tableau' table decoration. It was the **only** thing in that centre that held any reference to the true meaning of Christmas. A few years before I had been able to walk around and talk with my grandchildren about a life size model of Joseph with Mary on a donkey. Now we have life size singing reindeer, gnomes, loads of unicorns – all lit up – plus life size snowmen. This year too there seem to be ever more, and ever larger 'Santas', everywhere. The most recent one I've seen being a large blow up one sitting on a plane!!!!

Now I know that we have to come to terms with the fact that the world in which we live wants a mid-winter festival rather than a Christian celebration, driven as it is by commercial interest and competition, but for me the interesting thing is that the world still wants the peace and joy of which the angels sang. The world is looking for the great feelings of Christmas in the wrong place – in the shopping Mall and online buying – but we know where the peace and joy that they are looking for is found, and it is not in spending loads of money.

O.K. So now I hear you saying "this devotional is supposed to be about thanksgiving, what's going on?" I know, but I just had to have a little rant, and since we said yesterday that the angels must so enjoy our gratitude, I feel that they must look with great sadness at the state of our Christmas celebrations. It was, after all, the angels that first brought the message of peace and joy at Jesus' birth. It's a song that still echoes around our world, and they are still something for which most people long.

It was the angel of the Lord, breaking dramatically into our world, who said "I bring you good tidings of great joy, which shall be to all people". He gives the news about Jesus birth, and then a multitude of the heavenly host were there praising God and saying, "Glory to God in the highest, and on earth peace, good will toward men". (Luke 2:10,14, AV). How awesome, and how far, far away from our commercial Christmas today, but it doesn't have to be for us, who know why He came and what He did for us by coming into our world.

So as we approach Christmas, which literally means 'the feast of Christ', I am so grateful for a season that causes me to focus on that stupendous sacrifice; the one He made before going to the cross, the one where He 'Laid aside His Majesty, gave up everything for me.' The time when He, Jesus, 'Who, being in very nature God, did not consider equality with God a thing to be grasped, but made Himself **nothing**, taking the very nature of a servant, being made in human likeness. And being found in appearance as a man, he humbled himself and became obedient to death-even death on a cross!' (Philippians 2:6-8).

If the world is not going to be grateful to Him, I am! Please join me in this season. Instead of bemoaning the loss of a Holy season, let us intentionally give ourselves to thanking Jesus that He came into such a hostile world to die for us. Such love is incomprehensible, and I believe that as we join the angels, and give ourselves to thanking Him that He came – He didn't have to, but He came – the wonder of Christmas will be there for us, not because we have lots of coloured lights (which I love by the way) but because God said "Let light shine out of darkness," and He made that light shine in our hearts 'to give us the light of the knowledge of the glory of God in the face of Christ.' (2 Corinthians 4:6). It is truly wonderful.

Activation ...

Some ask should we do Christmas at all? Some of us try to put Christ back into Christmas by getting our friends and neighbours to a carol service, or we offer a meal to the homeless. Others of us try to navigate our way through by using the time to bless family and friends without overspending, or giving into the commercialism of the day.

This year let thanksgiving be your weapon of choice, enabling you to keep in close connection to the Lord so that whatever you do and however you celebrate this 'Feast of Christ' you do it in faith and to His honour in the glad company of the angels.

DAY 356 | Thanksgiving for Gifts Given Without my Having to be Good!

We spoke yesterday about the huge blown up, red Santa figures that appear all around us at this time of year. Our western Santa Claus has travelled a long way from the original St Nicholas of the 4th Century. He was a Saint who, tradition has it, did many good things and whose legacy has been embellished by many legends and by many different cultural appearances. In the nationalgeographic.com/history/article/131219[1] I read, 'It wasn't until the late 19th century, that the image of Santa became standardised as a full-size adult, dressed in red, with white fur trim, venturing out from the North Pole in a reindeer-driven sleigh and *keeping an eye on children's behavior.*' And so we have it, the gifts for 'good' children mythology is thrown in too.

Most of the characteristics of Father Christmas, (many of them American) were added because people love to surprise and bless their children in magical ways. So we have this strange state of affairs where Christmas has become all about gifts, not from God but from 'the man in red', and where two of the main questions that children are asked these days are, "What are you getting from Father Christmas this year?" and "Have you been good?"

I was contrasting that with Jesus' birth and I fell to thinking about the wise men, (not kings, and probably not three), who brought with them treasures to give this, by then, young child. He was the one whom they recognised as "the king of the Jews", (Matthew 2:1-11). It is such a beautiful scene. '... they saw the child with his mother Mary, and **they bowed down and worshipped Him**. Then they opened their treasures and presented him with gifts of gold and of incense and of myrrh.' Every one of those gifts had significance. Gold signifying Kingship, Frankincense, used in worshipping God, and Myrrh, indicating death and mortality; and as they gave those gifts they worshipped. For them it was about honouring this new King and what they were 'giving', not what they were 'getting' from Him.

Thinking about that scene I was reminded of one of the most profound Christmas sermons that I ever heard. It was given many years ago by David

Pawson. He got us to write down on a piece of paper (left for us on our seats) what we were going to 'give' to Jesus that Christmas. Immediately my thoughts went to things like 'my time', 'some money', 'my future plans', etc, but David directed us to pray and think more carefully, and to 'give' Jesus what He came for; the things that we normally hide, the things that spoil our lives, like our sin, our anger, our doubts and unbelief, our fears. He helped us to see that we could bless God by giving Him our bad stuff, and receiving from Him, His gifts of new life, of forgiveness, of joy and peace, of freedom – His good stuff.

The central scripture for me at Christmas is John 3:16. 'For God so loved the world that **He gave** His one and only Son, that whoever believes in him shall not perish but have eternal life.' The heart of this season is about remembering that incredible gift that God has given us in Jesus; in His coming into our world to die for us, in order to give us Salvation, a new life here on earth and an eternal life that will continue beyond death. There never can be, or ever will be, a greater gift than that. I am so thankful that God so loved the world that He **gave** His only Son, not for the 'good' girls and boys, but for the sinners. He came to seek and save the lost. (Luke 19:10). So I am thankful that I get what I don't deserve; gifts from my wonderful heavenly Father, not just at Christmas but every day of my life, whether I have been good or not.

I am also very thankful that I can give God gifts too. I can, as Christina Rossetti's lovely carol ends, 'Give Him my heart', and I can also give Him all the things that He died for, my bad stuff; it's all His anyway because He has bought it all with a price. Finally, like the wise men I can bring my gift of worship, and bring my 'thanks' to bless Him freely and often.

Activation . . .

Make this Christmas season a time of extravagant 'Thanksgiving' to the Lord. Overflow with thankfulness in each and every moment of it. Resist the moans and groans of the hassled and harried ones all around you, and declare out loud the reason for your thankfulness at this time. Let the fruit of your lips, honour Him thereby giving your family, friends and neighbours much food for thought at this time.

DAY 357 | Thanksgiving the Antidote to Perfectionism

It's funny, isn't it how we human beings, who are so full of failings, and so prone to make mistakes, often have in our heads a 'driving voice' that says "This has got to be perfect."? This can be true of a 'one off' special day like a wedding, a celebratory party, or the holiday of a lifetime and it can spill over into so many things in life, especially Christmas. Everything has got to be 'just right' if we are going to enjoy ourselves. We heard recently of a man who was making a round trip of around 40 miles in order to get a tree the right shape for his partner, because the one they had got was not 'right'.

While we can blame the media (yet again) for our 'drivenness' in these matters, it nevertheless becomes clear that the media is only tapping into an innate human weakness – that we all want certain things in life (and not just our church, or our partner!) to be perfect. Sure, it will be different things for different people, because we all have different 'perfectionist' drivers. For some at Christmas it's the externals like the food, the gifts and the decorations which need to be perfect; for others it's the relationships, and who visits who and for how long. Or maybe it will be about how smooth all the conversations are, and how all the interactions go.

The thing is, it's all about expectations and beliefs. My expectations of myself and of others; my beliefs that, in order to be enjoyed, Christmas should be 'perfect' in all the respects that I hold dear. The truth is, it hardly ever is perfect, is it? I even remember, as a child, coming to terms with the fact that my presents might be disappointing, and that my sister and I, however hard we tried, would probably have a quarrel and fall out at some point during the day. I realised then that, in order not to be disappointed, I needed to hold my ideal of a 'good day' very lightly indeed.

So what about the first Christmas? What a mess!! The awful political situation which caused a fully pregnant woman a most uncomfortable journey of 80 miles, probably on a horse or a donkey, all because a tyrant wanted a census to be taken. The crowds! No air B&B! No Travelodge or even a Macdonald's. Then when they finally find a shed in which to sleep and the baby is born, (no midwife available) the newborn ends up sleeping in the animal feeding trough. No pristine nursery here! How could God be so casual about the birth of His Son, the Saviour of the world? On the face of it, it all went so badly wrong, but there, in the midst of the muddle, chaos and imperfection, shone the Glory of God.

I just love it! I love the truth demonstrated here that the glory of God can shine in the midst of very messy situations, His glory can even shine in the midst of 'my mess'. God is perfect, but He is not a perfectionist. In Psalm 18:30 we read 'As for God **his way is perfect**; the word of the Lord is flawless. He is a shield for all who take refuge in Him.' Then a couple of verses further on we read, 'It is God who arms me with strength, **and makes my way perfect**.'

It's not the kind of perfection that we seek and long for in our material world, but it's the miracle of His ability to work out His purposes for us in the midst of very imperfect situations. **'He makes my way perfect'** because of His presence with me, and His interventions on my behalf. 'Messy' becomes 'perfect' because of His hand on my life and in my circumstances, as He works all things for my good. It is truly wonderful when I catch a glimpse of His mercy, grace and favour over my life, and how He uses every circumstance to make me more like Jesus. He just never gives up!

Activation ...

Thanksgiving in our 'messes' helps us to see above and beyond what is happening in the here and now. Thanksgiving helps us to go higher and see our situations from God's perspective, and His perspective is always glorious because He is glorious. He loves us and is so committed to doing us good in completely unbelievable ways; ways that the natural eye doesn't always see. Always thank God for His presence with you, even in the humanly speaking 'messy' moments of life, He will likely let you see something of what He is doing, and even share His joy over you, with you. This Christmas, whatever it holds, meditate on these words...

'The Lord your God is in your midst, A victorious warrior. He will exult over you with joy, He will be quiet in His love, He will rejoice over you with shouts of joy.' ... and stay thankful whatever happens. (Zephaniah 3:17, NASB).

DAY 358 | Thanksgiving on Christmas Day

This Christmas you may have many visitors, or none. You may be surrounded by family and friends, or you may be alone, separated from those you love by circumstances, difficulties or practicalities. You may be in good health or poor. You may be rich or poor, surrounded by gifts, or having none. There may be great quantities of delicious food on your table, or meagre rations.

Whatever your circumstances, I believe the Lord wants you to know that today – in Jesus – you have the most incredible present anyone could ever have, and that you are very, very rich. The Lord of Heaven and earth, with all that He is, and all that He can do, wants to be your 'Emmanuel' today. To each of us the richest measure of the divine presence is available. Remember those words from that wonderful carol 'O little Town of Bethlehem'[1] – 'Where meek souls will receive Him, still the dear Christ enters in'.

Today, I simply want to pray great blessing over you as, in whatever way is available to you, you celebrate the birth of our wonderful King of Kings.

I pray...

'May he grant you, out of the rich treasury of His glory to be strengthened *and* reinforced with mighty power in the inner man by the [Holy Spirit] [Himself indwelling in your innermost being and personality]. May Christ through your faith [actually] dwell, (settle down, abide, make His permanent home) in your hearts! May you be rooted deep in love *and* founded securely on love. That you may have the power *and* be strong to apprehend and grasp with all the saints [God's devoted people the experience of that love] what is the breadth and length and height and depth [of it]:

[That you may really come] to know [practically, through experience for yourselves] the love of Christ, which far surpasses mere knowledge [without experience]; that you may be filled [through all your being] unto all the fullness of God [may have the richest measure of the divine presence, and become a body wholly filled and flooded with God Himself]! (Ephesians 3:16-19, AMP).

Activation . . .

Whether it's busy or quiet where you are today, take some time to give Jesus your gifts of thanksgiving, praise and worship. Thank Him for coming and welcome Him again into your life afresh.

Make your thanksgiving heartfelt, not just words, (this is not a formula), let your thanks be given – in the words of another song, "from my heart to the heavens, Jesus be the centre. It's all about you. It's all about you."

And today may you receive with thanksgiving the gifts of great joy and great peace that His presence brings.

DAY 359 | Thanksgiving and Journaling

As I read Psalm 105 recently I felt it had something important to say to us as we come near to the end of our 365 days of looking at the power of thanksgiving. It had to do with the value of keeping a journal, and how that could be good for all of us, not just the natural writers and journal keepers. The Psalm starts with 'GIVE THANKS to the Lord, call on His name;' Now this is not a call to some sort of religious duty, but an invitation to a conversation within a relationship.

It is part, as we have previously noted, of keeping our 'intimate' relationship with the Lord alive and well. It's about 'acknowledging' Him or 'knowing' Him, in all our ways. This is really important to understand in our consideration of thanksgiving over the year. It is seeing that 'Thanksgiving is not some magic key, but rather a really important foundational part of our living, dynamic, ongoing, growing relationship with our Lord. Of course, like all of God's truths, it is also true that gratitude and thanksgiving will do every human being good, whether they have a saving faith or not. God knows how human beings tick and what is good for them. Thanksgiving is one of those things that, just like having a Sabbath day, does everyone good, atheists included.

So back to Psalm 105 and we see from the first few verses that thanksgiving and praise are part of a conversation and relationship with the Lord. This relationship includes seeking Him, and looking to Him for His strength on a daily basis. Then the Psalm continues in verse 5, 'Remember the wonders he has done, his miracles and the judgements he has pronounced . . .' And we have in the next 40 verses details of many of those things that God has done for them and His ways with them. It's like a journal of all God's goodness, faithfulness and working, in and around their lives, over many years.

On previous days we have shared how God makes it clear that when we forget, (and we are prone to forget) it can lead to trouble. We noted that remembering and not forgetting is so important to our faith and ongoing walk with the Lord. And so Psalm 105 leads us to the thought that keeping a journal of all that God is doing and of all that has come alive to me as I have read the bible; of all that He has done and said in the last week, last month and year will greatly aid my ongoing journey of thanksgiving.

I believe that an important key to journaling and flourishing faith is found in Zechariah 4:10. The context is important. The temple was destroyed, Jerusalem plundered, and then there was 70 years of exile. Now they are back and starting to rebuild the temple. The foundation has been laid. It's a small start. It's not looking anything like the glory of Solomon's temple, but God's word is **"Who despises the day of small things?** Men will rejoice when they see the plumb line in the hand of Zerubbabel." i.e. "The walls are beginning to go up." And note the preceding verses concerning this 'day of small things'. It's "'Not by might, nor by power, but by My Spirit", says the Lord Almighty' (verse 6). It's also about grace: 'He will bring forth the top stone with shouts of "Grace, grace to it,"' (verse 7).

You and I may read about past revivals, the book of Acts, or what is happening in church X or with sister Y, and feel that we have very little to shout about. They could have felt like that in Zechariah's day (see Haggai 2:3). In fact some of them wept because they remembered the glory of the former Temple. (See Ezra 3:12). So let us take on board God's word through Zechariah not to despise the day of small things, and fill our journals with 'small' blessings for which we can thank God; 'I found a parking space today', 'I had a lovely lunch', 'I had a friendly chat with my neighbour ', 'God encouraged me through a Psalm this morning.'

Machine guns are powerful and effective because they fire lots and lots of small bullets, small things, not one big boom. (Sorry for the illustration). And so lots and lots of little thanksgivings, day by day, are likely to lead to an explosion of grace, an increase in love for our wonderful Lord Jesus, deeper rest in our Father's love and growing confidence in the Holy Spirit within.

Activation ...

Let Jesus' words encourage you with this: "He (or She) who is faithful in a very little thing is faithful also in much . . ." (Luke 16:10, NASB). Don't say 'all I have seen is small' but get writing about all those small things in your journal **with thankfulness,** and let your journal greatly facilitate your ongoing growth in the Lord.

DAY 360 | Thanksgiving and Meditation

Yesterday we reflected on the value of a journal in facilitating a lifestyle of thanksgiving. As a post script to those thoughts it is important to differentiate between a journal and a diary. Diaries can often contain, and chronicle, many of the negatives of my current life without necessarily looking at the way forward and how to rise up and grow. Journals, will also record my battlegrounds, my tough times, my fears, struggles and defeats, but as a believer my journal will also be looking at what the Lord is doing and saying into my life, how my faith and walk with Him can grow, and how He is developing me, as His disciple, and working in all things for my good to make me more like Jesus. The Christian life was described as 'the way', (Acts 9:2, 19:23), and it is essentially my 'walk with God' (just like Enoch, see Genesis 5:22,24) that I am journaling. Journaling is about the journey.

Something that may help my journaling and, more generally, my 'walk' with the Lord is meditation. We hear a great deal in these days about the value of meditation and so as Christians we need to know that meditation is a biblical concept. Godly, biblical meditation is of great benefit to us, to our wellbeing and peace of mind, and also in our growth as believers. Don't believe that other religions invented meditation, David was on to it long before other religions and philosophies started advocating it. For example in Psalm 9:16 the verse concludes with, 'Higgaion, Selah'. Higgaion is a word that we are told in both the AV, NIV and Amplified margins, means 'meditation'. Even more wonderful is the Amplified Bible's expansion of the word 'Selah'. It means, 'pause and calmly think about that.'

This is a key to biblical meditation. It is not using something like music or chanting to empty your mind. Biblical meditation has been well described as being like a cow chewing the cud. You sit, stand, or walk, just like a cow, calmly chewing over (ruminating) on what the Lord, in His word, has said to you today, this week, or previously in your life. (see Matthew 13:52). Like the cow you regurgitate the good food from the Lord that you have eaten, through His word, over the days and weeks, and chew it over, extracting more sweet nourishment. 'Pause and calmly think about that'. Not 'pause and try and think about nothing'. Chewing on the 'that' which God has just spoken to you through His word is vital to healthy meditation. You don't see a cow chewing with an empty mouth!

Another helpful observation I heard many years ago from a great bible teacher was the idea that it is easy for the Holy Spirit to bring back to my memory and attention, when I need it, something that I have previously read, even memorised, from the Bible. If I have never read it, it is obviously 'harder' for the Holy Spirit to bring it to mind. So keep reading, even if there seems to be no great revelation at the time, as it will feed your future meditations! I often find that reviewing some of the things that I have previously noted in my journal is a great way forward. Reviewing, even meditating, on past 'words' can feed my faith for the day ahead.

In Psalm 104:34 we find a link between meditation, praise and thanksgiving. We read, 'May my meditation be pleasing to Him as I rejoice in the Lord.' It seems very likely that, as I meditate with a heart filled with thankfulness, the truths upon which I am 'chewing' will go deeper and have a more profound effect on my faith levels. Thanksgiving itself is closely allied to remembering the Lord's goodness and promises, and so healthy meditation will have a good deal of thanksgiving threaded all the way through it.

Meditation without thanksgiving can be vulnerable to intrusive negative thoughts because we can also, quite easily, meditate on the negatives of life. If we **forget to 'stay' our mind on the Lord**, our meditations can leave us wandering off in our minds down trails of discouragement, and diminishing faith. (Just saying!) Better by far to meditate with a heart of gratitude and be like the writer of the beautiful hymn who wrote, about 250 years ago, 'His love in times past, forbids me to think, He'll leave me at last in trouble to sink.'[1] I need to constantly remind myself of 'His love in time past' by chewing on it in thankful meditation so that I don't run the risk of 'forgetting' like the Israelites.

Activation ...

Today let your thanksgiving be entwined in your journaling, and let it also be a vital and ongoing fuel in all your meditations.

DAY 361 | Thanksgiving that Lifts Me Up

A few days ago we used the illustration of the accumulative effect of lots of small bullets being fired. We wrote that 'Lots and lots of little thanksgivings, day by day, are likely to lead to an explosion of grace, an increasingly passionate love for our wonderful Lord Jesus, deeper rest in our Father's love, and growing confidence in the Holy Spirit within.'

That got me thinking about the truth that often progress in life is made up of a lot of small steps. I remember as a child visiting the sights in central London and being taken to the Monument, the 202 foot tower that was built to mark the Great Fire of London of 1666. At the time of building it was a very tall building, and obviously had no lift. No way to get to the top other than by climbing the 311 steps. For me as a small child this was quite an adventure in itself, counting and climbing all the steps and discovering the view of London from the top.

Living in the age of high speed lifts, we are used to rising to the top of a high rise building in no time at all, but there is still no way of getting to the top of the Monument except by rising up step by step. When tourists come to climb The Monument you don't hear anyone say, "Well that bottom step is useless, it won't get me anywhere near the top." Because everyone knows that stepping onto the bottom step and then the next and then the next is the only way to go up. Maybe we could apply this to ourselves as Christians. Perhaps sometimes we want to take the lift, not the steps, in our spiritual life, so we go to a big meeting, or connect with one on youtube, and we feel our spirit lift quite soon or even immediately. If we haven't climbed the steps however, but have metaphorically whizzed to the top in a lift, we may find ourselves coming down again very quickly!

Let us put this in some kind of context. Some days we may start off the day feeling challenged by the day ahead, or out of sorts with God, others, or even ourselves. On other days we can start well, but there may be setbacks and difficulties arising along the way. Whatever the cause, we can sometimes feel like the challenges of the day are too much for us, or that the Lord seems far away. It can feel more like being at the bottom of the

Monument where we can't see the magnificent view, rather than at the top: More as if we are under the circumstances rather than riding high as one who Christ 'always leads in triumph' and through whom, 'the fragrance of the knowledge of God (is spread) everywhere.' (2 Corinthians 2:14 AMP).

So what do we do if on this day, like at the Monument, there is no high speed lift to transport us upwards? Then I think our daily discipline of 'giving thanks in all things' is the answer and a little like those 311 steps that have to be taken one by one to get to the top. Thanksgiving, as we have now said so many times, is vital in building a healthy spiritual life and a strong connection with our Heavenly Father. I think it can also be our 'step by step' movement 'upwards' when we are feeling in any way 'down'. Like the many small bullets mentioned, or the steps of the Monument, giving thanks for a lot of little things is a great way to 'lift' our spirit.

At those times of feeling 'down' or 'under the circumstances' we can find it hard to remember all the good things that the Lord has done for us. Sometimes, even when we do remember something, the enemy will be there whispering, 'Was that really God? Or was it just one of those things?' thereby attempting to lead us into a measure of doubt and unbelief. And this is where we come back to keeping it very simple, and not 'despising the day of small things', in the same way that we would in no way despise the bottom step(s) at the Monument if we wanted to get to the top.

This is where our journal can help us. Re reading that list of 'small things' that we have written down for which we are thankful (see Day 359 again), can provide us with the steps that we need to climb back into a place where we can clearly see the view; that is to say a place in the Spirit, where we can gain God's perspective on our day, and our circumstances, once again.

Activation . . .

Determine in your heart today to resist all temptation to 'give up' on 'Giving Thanks' and practice using thanksgiving like small steps the next time you are feeling something like, 'This is all too much!' or even 'This thanksgiving isn't getting me high enough fast enough.'

DAY 362 | Thanksgiving to Build Myself Up

There are several encouragements in the New Testament to 'build ourselves up'. Paul writes to the Christians in Colossae telling them to be 'being continually built up in Him, becoming increasingly more confirmed *and* established in the faith, just as you were taught, and abounding *and* overflowing in it **with thanksgiving**'. (Colossians 2:7, AMP). Jude, in verse 20 of his letter, also encourages us with the words, '... build yourselves up in your most holy faith and pray in the Holy Spirit.'

Building doesn't have to, but often does, imply putting lots of small elements together, and we have recently been thinking about the combined effect of a lot of small things together. We looked at the numerous small steps that help us to go up to a great height; then there is also the picture of all the small drops of rain that can end up soaking us through and through. So combining that thought about the effect of lots of small things and 'building ourselves up', my mind turned to thinking about a very strong wall that is made up of lots of small bricks.

The strongest of buildings, those that can last for centuries, often have walls made of hundreds and thousands of relatively small bricks, or blocks of stone, the combined strength of which can mean that it will require a bulldozer or a wrecking ball to demolish it. Now clearly those bricks, in order to stay connected and to stay strongly in place, need to be put together with some good mortar. I then got to thinking how this principle could apply to 'building ourselves up in our most holy faith'.

Now stay with me here! If we think of each brick as something that the Lord has done for us in terms of our walk with Him in the practicalities of life, then each thing does not have to be huge in itself to be part of the building. Building myself up in order that I become 'established in my faith' can, and indeed must, include acknowledging and remembering the small daily things that God does, as well as my salvation, the big deliverances and the big moments in my life. Additionally 'building' implies a step by step growth; as the famous saying goes, 'Rome was not built in a day'.

The foundational stones for our faith building will be the big things that God has done for us like Jesus' death on the cross, God's love and kindness in searching us out, the miracle of 'New Birth' by His Spirit and the truth that we have been given a new nature. Then there is the fact that we are totally forgiven, and the life changing blessing of the indwelling Holy Spirit, and let's not forget the huge and unfathomable inheritance, kept in heaven for us that will be ours to enjoy for all eternity. Jesus is **the** foundation stone of our life and faith, (1 Corinthians 3:4), and then all these wonderful things that God has done will be the additional foundations upon which we 'build ourselves up'.

Then day by day, brick by brick, we can build upon these foundations as we recognise and absorb God's love for us in all those daily mercies and blessings, in all those truths that we read in the Bible day by day, and in all the daily provision that we receive for our body, mind and spirit. Then there is the day to day friendship and fellowship with the Lord; His daily leading and guiding. As I recognise and acknowledge all of these wonderfully kind interventions in my life, they become the bricks with which I can build myself up in my faith.

In this context thanksgiving is like the mortar that connects and holds all these 'bricks' from my daily life experiences together. It is like the cement that holds together lots of small bricks of blessing to make a very strong wall of defense around my heart, mind and spirit. This is most important because it is about building up my spiritual resilience and strength. If I have been building myself up day by day, with thanksgiving for all that the Lord does and has done for me, when the enemy tries to demolish me by sending in a wrecking ball, (and he will), then I will have more resilience against the doubts and fears with which the enemy would assail me.

Activation ...

Today make a point of doing what those verses that we quoted earlier from Colossians and from Jude suggest. Build yourself up in faith as you 'pray in the Spirit' and **overflow with thanksgiving**. Ask the Holy Spirit to keep you aware of the Lord's presence in your life from the smallest to the biggest mercy and blessing. Decide to get building day by day, and make sure that you are ready and strong in the storms of life, if and when they come.

DAY 363 | Thanksgiving and Seeing His Face

We were in a different church on Sunday, a church with a small congregation. I was sitting at the back (the chairs were more comfortable there!) and so because I was looking at the back of people's heads, I recognised very few of them. No surprise then that I felt very little connection with anybody. Unconnected, that was, until afterwards over a cup of coffee when I fell to talking with a few who recognised me. As we chatted their welcome, and the warmth of their smiles, gave me a very different picture of that little community. Everyone looked very different face to face. I saw pleasure and kindness, sorrow, and pain, joy and even 'faith' in the different faces. Suddenly my joy at being there significantly increased as I saw different ones of them face to face.

There is so much we can see in a face, and it got me thinking about David's use of the word 'face'. There is no Hebrew word for 'presence', and so when he wants to speak of God's presence he uses the Hebrew word for 'face', (Psalm 16:11). The literal translation is, "you fill me with joy as we come face to face." When we 'see' someone's face, catch their eye, see their smile, they suddenly become 'present' to us. We know this because the converse is also true. If someone doesn't want to invite us into their 'presence', they don't give us eye contact, or they 'freeze us out', maybe even turning right away from us.

The apostle Paul wrote 'For God, who commanded the light to shine out of darkness, hath shined in our hearts to *give* the light of the knowledge of **the glory of God in the face of Jesus Christ**.' (2 Corinthians 4:6, AV). So, in the light of this truth, let's look again at the incredible blessing that the Lord directed Aaron, through Moses, to speak over the Israelites, "The Lord bless you and keep you; the Lord make **His face to shine upon you and be gracious to you; the Lord turn His face towards you and give you peace.**" (Numbers 6:24-26) Wow! Read that again very slowly. I feel His presence and pleasure even as I type that out!

I believe that every time we give thanks from our heart, it's like we lift our face to His and He turns His face towards us and we know that He is smiling, if not even singing, over us. (see Zephaniah 3:17) Then look at what God says next, He says that if the priests will speak blessing over the children of Israel in this way, "So they will put my name on the Israelites, and I will bless them." (Numbers 6:27). His face, His name, His presence, His blessing, let's have it all.

So if giving thanks is the equivalent of turning my face (my heart) to His, in order to connect deeply with Him, then there is something here that I need to see. I must see that there is a difference between the 'thank you' that I give the person at the supermarket as I pay for my shopping and the 'thank you' that I give a little grandchild who has painstakingly drawn me a picture, or made me a card. The former I may not even notice as I go on my way, especially if I am running late!! To my grandchild, on the other hand, I will give my full attention, catch their eye and smile, conveying my delight and pleasure over the gift and, by way of acknowledging the effort put in, I will express in detail what it is about the picture that I love. The connection is then complete. The child also smiles, glowing with happiness as she receives the affection and affirmation coming her way.

So now we can see how that this whole year of thanksgiving has been about turning our hearts and faces towards Him, about seeing His face a little more clearly day by day. It has not been about a simple formula, but about making and keeping a deeper, stronger connection with the Almighty. I know that I will need to revisit some, maybe many, of these devotionals and repent of any time when my thanksgiving has been formulaic. I don't want to take for granted this precious gift of 'thanksgiving'; this simple way we have of gaining immediate access into His presence.

Activation . . .

Join me now in giving thanks again and again for this beautiful way of coming face to face with Him. This is where we started this journey, around a year ago now. (Book 1, Day 1). We started with Psalm 100:4, (so unforgettable) **'Come right into His presence with thanksgiving. Come bring your thank offering to Him and affectionately bless His beautiful name!'** (from The Passion Translation) or in effect, **'Come face to face with God as you give Him your heartfelt thanks in all and every situation.'**

DAY 364 | Thanksgiving and Transformation

Yesterday we were looking at how our heartfelt thanksgiving can bring us into God's presence, **'face to face'** with our Lord. This whole year we have sought to thank God in so many different ways, in so many different situations, (the good, the bad and the ugly!!) for the many, many different ways in which He blesses us, and reveals who He is to us. Through this time, as we have chosen to offer up our thanks (at times as a sacrifice), we have been deepening our friendship with Him. Thanksgiving brings us this heart to heart connection with Him – and it also changes us! And it is this mystery that we are going to consider today.

Paul tells us that we are transformed into His likeness as 'we all with **open face beholding** as in a glass the glory of the Lord are changed into the same image from glory to glory, even as by the Spirit of the Lord.' (2 Corinthians 3:18, AV). The apostle John also tells us, 'Dear friends, now we are children of God, and what we will be has not yet been made known. But we know that when He appears **we shall be like Him for we shall see Him as He is.**' (1 John 3:2). There is definitely something about 'seeing Jesus', seeing our wonderful Messiah, that causes us to become like Him. Amazing!

Now as I ponder this it makes perfect sense for, even in our natural world, when someone gives us something good, it doesn't just evoke gratitude in our hearts, it alters our disposition towards that person. We become aware of them in a new way, we 'see' them in a new light. When someone gives me a gift and I express my appreciation for it, it disarms me, I let down some of my reserve and welcome them a little deeper into my life.

Over the past year, as we have sought to approach the Lord with gratitude at every turn, our appreciation for Him, His love, His sacrifice for us, His gifts to us, (incredible generosity), His commitment to do us good at all times and in all circumstances, rises meteorically. The staggering truth that the God of all creation is my loving Heavenly Father, and calls me His beloved child, becomes more and more real.

Expressing my gratitude to Him as I notice, and become more aware of, His love and interventions in my life, helps to open me up to see Him more fully in His glory. I see His kindness, goodness, love, forgiveness, faithfulness, patience and strength, spread out before me like the colours of a vivid rainbow. And as I behold His beauty, 'the sweet attractiveness and the delightful loveliness of the Lord' (Psalm 27:4, AMP), little by little, because I am liking and enjoying what I see, I am transformed from within by the Spirit and I then, when I am with other people, start to behave more and more like Jesus would if He were in my place.

Even though 'Now we see but a poor reflection as in a mirror; then shall we see face to face. Now I know in part; then I shall know fully, even as I am fully known.' (1 Corinthians 13:12), the process of change happens as I 'look at Jesus'. So the more I thank Him, the more I have a lifestyle of gratitude, the closer I seem to get to the Lord. Now in some ways we can't get any closer to Him, He is always very close to us in our world, but thanksgiving lets me into His world, and I see Jesus enthroned; I see the Father's love and the Holy Spirit's constant working in my life in richer colour than before. Then the more that I see and comprehend of my amazing Triune God, the more I am changed to be like Him, and the more I reflect who He is into the world.

His intention for us is that we should 'shine'. He said 'I am the light of the world' and also that we are 'the light of the world'. He told us to let that light shine before men. (Matthew 5:14-16). So, as you continue to develop a life of thanksgiving, ponder those wonderful words that Isaiah spoke to God's people around two and a half thousand years ago, "ARISE, SHINE for your light has come, and the glory of the Lord rises upon you. See, darkness covers the earth and thick darkness is over the peoples, but the Lord rises upon you and his glory appears over you. Nations will come to your light, and kings to the brightness of your dawn." (Isaiah 60:1-3).

Activation . . .

Determine with me to keep on growing your heart of 'thanksgiving', so that you can keep on beholding Him, and so keep on shining for Him.

DAY 365 | Our Year of Thanksgiving and God's Open Door

So here we are on Day 365 of our 'Thanksgiving Journey'. From day one we saw afresh that 'Thanksgiving' is a key to entering the courts of Heaven. Whilst the Lord is always with us, 'Thanksgiving' is a key to experiencing the Lord's presence and to being able to stand confidently before His throne of grace. It is also a key to receiving, not just salvation, but all the resources that we need to walk through life as citizens of Heaven.

It is also a vital key to understanding things from God's perspective, and to be able to live a different way. Living from above. It is a big key to seeing myself as God sees me, pure and holy, and then it's the key to appropriating the truth that God works all things for my good and uses every circumstance to transform me little by little into the likeness of Jesus. (Romans 8:28-30).

I think one of the precious truths that I have discovered is this. Thanksgiving is more than a key, it's like the knock on the door of heaven that says, "Papa, I'm here to chat". Now let me explain that a little more. Over this past month I have found many questions going through my mind that I would like God to answer. Questions ranging from the big powerful questions like, "Why is there so much suffering in the world?" to the smaller questions like, "What do you want me to do in this, or that, situation?"

What I have found is this; that any conversation with the Lord that starts with me asking a 'what' 'where', 'when' or 'why' question feels like hard work. These questions start any conversation with the Lord from my earth bound perspective, and so it can feel like wading through treacle as I try to bring my thoughts into line with His. I think this is because my thoughts and feelings make it hard to hear Holy Spirit with my spirit.

When however, I come into His presence with a 'thank you', "Thank you Lord for X,Y or Z, . . ." "Thank you Lord that you have all the wisdom that I need . . ." "Thank you Lord for your love and care," "Thank you Lord that you know what I need to do now . . ." etc, I find that my spirit takes the lead. Then, as I share my thoughts and questions, the Holy Spirit can impart more of

God's wisdom into my spirit. Then my mind and my heart can better grasp His ways.

God says 'My door is always open', and unlike many a manager or leader who says that because they have learnt that good leaders say these things, God's door really **is** always open. The picture that He gave me was of 'thanksgiving' being like a knock on the door. Not a locked front door, but more like a Narnia type scenario where a young Lucy approaches the old Professor's study door. The door is ajar, but closed enough to stop the child from rushing in. Her knock on the door is however in itself enough to swing the door open on its well oiled hinges, revealing a warm welcoming room and the professor ready to talk and answer her questions.

It's a picture showing us that God's door is always open to us, and a simple 'knock' – my 'Thanksgiving', swings it wide. As we, God's children, knock on His half opened door with our thanksgiving, He welcomes us with joy. We can approach Him freely, and the conversations that we have with Him then are of a different calibre, and more like the conversations that Jesus had with His disciples on earth – full of wisdom and truth.

God's invitations to **'come'**, ring out through the Bible. '**Come** all you who are thirsty, **come** to the waters; and you who have no money, **come**, buy and eat! **Come** buy wine and milk without money or cost.' (Isaiah 55:1). **Come** to me, all who are weary and burdened and I will give you rest...' (Matthew 11:28). '**Come** follow me.' (Matthew 19:21), and of course, 'If anyone is thirsty, let him **come** to me and drink...' (John 7:37).

There is absolutely no doubt, God wants us to **come** to Him, anytime, anywhere, just as we are. His door is open. Let us always now approach Him like little children, knocking on His door with our 'thanksgiving'. Let us see how, as we approach Him in this way, the door swings wide as He welcomes us into His presence again and again. Whether we come to talk things over with Him, to worship, to present our requests, to share our burdens, or to receive from Him whatever it is we need at that moment, let us remember that **we are always welcome**, and so let us make this our 'Psalm 100:4' lifestyle and always...

<u>**'Enter His gates with thanksgiving and His courts with praise;**</u>
<u>**give thanks to Him and praise His name**</u>.

What next?

As before, we pray that, as you have read and pondered these daily devotionals, you will have absorbed some more of the relentless love that God has for you, and that you have been drawn closer to Him day by day.

For some the four books may take you through a year, others may find it helpful to travel through the books more slowly, taking longer.

I believe there will be lasting benefit in reading through all four books in a regular rhythm, at the pace that suits you best, we are all different.

If you would like to purchase further copies of any of the four books then please email us at:-

enquiries@lifetraining.co.uk.

Notes

Day 277
1. 10,000 Reasons (Bless the Lord). Matt Redmond, Jonas Myrin Copyright © 2011 Thankyou Music (Admin. by EMI Christian Music Publishing)

Day 281
1. John Mark Comer The Ruthless Elimination of Hurry. Hodder and Stoughton 2019.
2. Carl Jung. Quotefancy.com accessed online 20.11.2023
3. Corrie ten Boom. quote by John Mark Comer as above

Day 292
1. God I look to You. Jenn Johnson / Ian Mcintosh © Bethel Music Publishing

Day 293
1. Lord I Come to You. Geoff Bullock Copyright © 1992 Word Music/ Maranatha! Music/adm. Unisong/Universal.

Day 296
1. Adrian Plass. The Sacred Diary of Adrian Plass Aged 37. Harper Collins 1987

Day 304
1. Warren Buffett says this 1 simple habit separates successful people from everyone else. Marcel Schwantes on 'getpocket' on line downloaded 2.10.21

Day 305
1. C S Lewis. The Problem of Pain. Harper Collins 1993.

Day 314
1. Wait on You. Brandon Lake / Chandler Moore / Chris Brown / Dante Bowe / Steven Furtick / Tiffany Hudson © Bethel Music Publishing, Capitol Christian Music Group, Sony/ATV Music Publishing LLC

Day 316
1. When we walk with the Lord. (Trust and Obey) John H Sammis

Day 321
1. Jesus at the Centre. Israel Houghton, Micah Massey, Adam Ranney. Copyright © 2015 Maranatha! music

Day 326
1. Let us give thanks Brian Howard Copyright © 1974 The Fisherman, Inc.

Day 329
1. Nothing Hidden ministries. Love after Marriage. Nothinghidden.org.uk, nothinghidden.com/love-after-marriage/

Day 338
1. Take my life and let it be. Frances Ridley Havergal

Day 345
1. Here I am. Martin Smith & Stuart Garrard Copyright © 2003 Curious? Music UK/Bucks Music Ltd

Day 348
1. The 5 love languages. Gary Chapman. 1992 Northfield publishing

Day 353
1. Hark the herald-angels sing. Charles Wesley

Day 356
1. nationalgeographic.com/history/article/131219
2. In the bleak mid winter. Christina Rossetti

Day 358
1. O little town of Bethlehem. Phillips Brooks

Day 360
1. Begone Unbelief, my Saviour is near. John Newton